Number People

By Dawn Cornelius

NUMBER PEOPLE

Copyright © 2014 by Dawn Cornelius

Copyright fuels creativity, encourages diverse voices, promotes free speech, and creates a vibrant culture and platform for ideas. Thank you for purchasing an authorized edition of this book and for so graciously complying with copyright laws by not reproducing, scanning, or distributing any part of it in any form without permission.

ISBN 978-0-9910574-0-5

While the author has made every effort to provide accurate contact information at the time of publication, neither the publisher nor the author assumes any responsibility for errors or changes that occur after publication.

All cover designs by Adam Richards.

To Grandmomma,
I never knew love like this before.

"There is no greater agony than bearing an untold story inside you." Maya Angelou

Acknowledgements

There are so many people who deserve to be thanked.

Thank you God for the life you have given me, the joy it has brought me, and the glory it will give you.

Thank you Michael, my husband of almost 12 years at the time this book is published. You are an important and invaluable part of my story and I can only pray that our union and nearly 12 years together have been a treasured and blessed part of your life as it has mine. Our story has not been wasted.

To Olivia, Kristian, and Ezra, you are the best ones and I still can't believe that out of all the children in the world...I was given the best ones. I love you eternally beyond measure. I am grateful for the story you're writing with your lives.

Jordan, you are my beloved...forever.

Scott, this book would not be possible without you. Thank you for the countless hours spent helping to bring my voice to paper. Thank you for your faith in me and in this project. You are a master craftsman of words, gifted more than you know, and I have come to know you as my friend. I treasure you.

Adam, you are gracious, brilliant, and gifted in all your ways. I am constantly thankful for you, your contributions to this project editorially, as a designer, as a marketer, and mostly as a friend. Your sacrifice never goes unnoticed. Thank you.

Christina, thank you for your time and talent on this book. I appreciate your friendship. I value you.

Beverly, the timing of your arrival in my life could only be described and understood by realizing nothing happens by coincidence. You are a gift in so many ways. Thank you for the all the ways you have given life to me and to this project. I'm extremely grateful for you.

Thank you Clarice. It's even in your death that you give me hope and courage. Nikia, Joi, Asia...you three are so much more than the fruit of her labor. I treasure you.

My sister friends are my strength, conscience, and solace. Brenda and Karen, you have been faithful "rocks." I thank God for you.

My godchildren, Breion, Jamiliah, Jada, and Jeremiah, you are eternally loved.

Shawn, I love you. You are my brother and my friend.

My family, you are numerous and strong, I love you. Thank you for shaping my story.

Contents

Foreword   14

How to Use this Book   18

Part One: My Story

One   21
Arthur Avenue

Two   43
A Chariot Swung Low

Three   65
Perfectly Losers

Four   98
Abandoning Camelot

Five   122
Good Begets Good

Part Two: Your Story

Six   153
Plot: Your Number is a Catalyst

Seven   175
Character: Your Number Changes Your Relationships

Eight   197
Conflict: Your Number Can Bring Healing

Nine   217
Resolution: Your Number Determines Your Outcome

Part Three: A Bigger Story   232

About the Author   242

Foreword

It's 6 a.m. In the background, an American Airlines safety video just thanked me for my attention. But I'm a million miles away. My attention is somewhere else.

I'm on a flight to Haiti. It's the first trip I have taken overseas to see the work being accomplished through the partnerships my company has created. I'll be visiting an orphanage there and spending time with abandoned children. After a short layover in Miami, my feet will be on the ground there for the first time.

Yesterday, August 23, my father died. In the moments after his death, I looked at my phone wanting to inscribe in my mind the date…and sighed to myself when I realized that once again, the number 23 had taken a transformative place in my life history.

Numbers are a universal language we all speak. No matter who you are or where you come from, we all have numbers that serve as markers, as trophies, that tell the unique testimony of our life's journey. 1907, 1930, 1972, 1990, 1992, 2005…the numbers vary, they mean different things to each of us, but all of us with a life story have one thing in common:

We all have a number.

As you explore this new concept, I want to personally declare you as one of the Number People.

This book began nearly 20 years ago, when I first knew I had a book inside me. But it has taken years for it to mature in my heart. I hope you are as inspired as I have been in the process of writing it.

My dream is that I will one day overhear a conversation between a boyfriend quizzing a date about the numbers that most impacted her life, a father sharing with his daughter why the year of her birth is inked on his wrist, a student introducing herself to her first grade teacher with the year she will graduate from college, or a terrified new entrepreneur gathering his team for the first time around the number that led him to that courageous decision.

Numbers are all around us. But *our* numbers are inside us.

Over the course of the chapters ahead, I'm going to introduce you to my story and how the numbers throughout my life have served as weapons of hope during tough and arduous days. I want to show you how we all have these life-changing numbers and how these numbers can change our life stories. I want to convince you that there is something extraordinary in all of our lives that when seen, understood, and harnessed can become powerful assets and can help us to make sense of the world in ways that other things cannot.

***

"Life-changing" is an interesting word. Most people are intimidated by it. When used to describe an event, it often casts a bigger-than-life spell over the moment to suggest that the skies split and the universe somehow shook with a "life-changing" force.

When using this definition, most people will immediately exclaim, "I don't have one."

But the universe doesn't have to shake on its axis nor do the stars twinkle in delight for a moment in your life to bring change, purpose, and shape to it. In a society driven by bigger and better glitz, we have somehow lost affection for the small and overlooked moments that are a different kind of life-changing. Moments that when looked back upon later served to change the trajectory of our lives in one way or another. We all have these moments. Every opportunity, every decision, no matter how small, has the seeds within it to become life-changing.

Every moment has the chance to be a number that will change your life.

These numbers we hold are for us, but not just for us. I pray that you are encouraged and inspired as you read this book, that you will contemplate your life more seriously, yet more playfully and more thoughtfully, and that you will be pushed into action to use the moments that have impacted you most to help others.

We are the Number People. We are the ones who see more than the digits. We are the ones who own something special inside us and along with it the responsibility to pass it on. We are the ones who see hope rather than coincidence; courage rather than chance. I am a Number Person because of some very impactful people who changed my life. And as I reckon with that, and come to terms with what it means for the rest of my life, I am looking for others to come alongside me.

I'm excited to journey ahead with you!

Dawn

How to Use This Book

This book is written in three parts with three different intentions.

Part One, My Story, tells the story of how I came to hold some very special numbers on my heart, and how those numbers got me through some incredibly dark days.

Part Two, Your Story, is written to help you discover the number you hold on your heart, and how it can change every element of the life story you are writing: your plot, your characters, your conflict, and your resolution.

Part Three, A Bigger Story, is written to challenge you to consider your legacy. The point of this book is to usher you in to this bigger story—to remind you that in your final moments, all alone or with your family gathered around, after your possessions are divvied up, your assets sold, and your loose ends tied, your legacy will be the last thing you have. In a matter of seconds, in a handful of heartbeats, you will go from a person people know to a person they remember. And all they'll have to go on is the legacy you leave. You have left a number on their hearts they'll carry to the world.

Included online are some practical helps for you as you work through this process, or as you lead others through this process. For additional resources and support, we have set up an online community at dawncornelius.com.

My hope is that this book will change the way you look at your life and those who have impacted it. You are not alone in this journey. Seek help, find accountability, form a community of likeminded seekers you can work through this process with.

Life was not meant to be experienced alone. This book isn't either.

Part One

My Story

One

Arthur Avenue

I was thirty the first time I saw the plantation. My grandmother had been gone more than a decade then and our family divorced from the sharecropping life for half a century. By 2002, I was long baptized in family pride over where we came from, and how Witherspoon roots run deep into the Alabama soil, and the clamor and propulsion of my own thirty-something life afforded me a noble distance from it several hours north in Nashville. I knew what our family history in Alabama meant. I knew the pride we held in it. But I didn't really need to see it.

In my mind I had already seen the plantation, every time my grandmother stroked my hair and recounted their Depression lives, offering story after story of how it was all something worth being proud of, somehow, because our family had been cast a certain lot in a certain place in history, and because of our willingness to face it and overcome it and then own it, I could have the life I wanted. I had walked plantation soil hundreds of times in my head, drifting down wet rows of cotton and sulking in the shadows of stately magnolias as her fingers traced across my temples. She made it real for me. She made *sure* it was real for me. I didn't need to see Alabama. I already held my own vision of it.

This had always been enough, so that summer when my Aunt Ada asked me to drive her and my father to a family reunion there, I would have done anything not to go. What could be there for me? What else was there to gain? They had all chosen to leave the state one by one decades ago, chasing their own educational and entrepreneurial dreams in Tennessee in the 1940s and '50s and because of that I saw my path already carved out for me. I was already well down it, successful and distracted and busy. That path didn't lead back to Alabama.

I already knew well the bones of our family, that my grandmother was born in Alabama in 1907 and sharecropped there alongside her husband Bestedia and four children on a dusty plantation, selling whatever they grew to piece together what life they could during the Depression. They were poor, always. Just about everyone in the rural county they were from was back then. The way they fought against it was with their own inventiveness and entrepreneurial spirit, and that's where our pride was rooted. Sharecropping was never enough. There was something inside them that drove them to work for more. And one by one the children expressed it, running loads of chopped wood into town to sell for nickels, and peddling ice around town from a truck when they were just twelve years old. This ambition they held would eventually bubble over and carry them right off the plantation and out of Alabama altogether. They created a kind of freedom for themselves, and it took them to small businesses they would own all over Tennessee, a lifetime away from the Alabama dirt. This momentum, this feeling that there was always something more to reach toward would shape their lives. I would eventually come to know where it came from, because the woman who birthed it in them didn't stop when those children were up and gone.

She married Bestedia in 1923, sixteen years old and two decades his junior, and it might have looked scandalous if they didn't love each other so much. Lula came first in 1927, when my grandmother was just twenty, then Ada in 1929. My father, James, came the next year, and Uncle Ben followed in 1931. Five years, four kids, six mouths, one plot of land, and one Great Depression in the background of it all. The simple arithmetic for a sharecropping family just trying to make it one day to the next.

Olivia Witherspoon was the rock of her family's world the same way she would later become the rock of mine. She labored alongside them, sharing their sacrifice and struggle season after season just to survive. But those lives were so different from mine. I knew them through wistful stories and washed out photographs. But I knew her as something real and in my version of her she was just grandmomma. She had come to mean something different to me than she did to her children. Every one of them, from Lula to Ada to James to Ben, clawed to get out of Alabama, to find schools and work in Tennessee and leave these parts of their past behind them. It felt like they had earned something that had simply been given to me.

My only trips to Alabama to that point were as a little girl, when midnight rides to nameless funerals had been dozed away in the backseat as we dissected the state's roads. Still, out of a sense of guilt or obligation, or maybe both, I agreed to a quick trip—*Five hours in, five hours out*, I told myself—but after the reunion was over, as I walked Aunt Ada and my father gingerly back to the car, the plan to come right back changed with a simple request. Before we headed home, they said, they wondered if we could see the place they had spent their childhood.

I had never seen those fields before. They were almost mythical to me, existing only in bedtime stories set far, far away. But the two of them wore it differently. Aunt Ada had just lost her husband, the man who brushed her hair and cooked her breakfast and laid out her clothes when her eyesight went after the stroke. It was the first time I "really" saw her without Uncle Harris, and as we drove toward the house I could see she was thoughtful and reflective and sad.

Soon the roads leading into the plantation drew us deep into the country, stuck to the hills and curves of the land like typewriter ribbon wound through pine trees and cracked pasture. The tires popped over hot gravel that gave way to dusty red clay as we neared the plots of land they once spent part of their childhood. I parked in the gravel and helped them out. Soon we began to wander, losing the afternoon along the paths the two of them had marked as children step for step.

Aunt Ada held my arm as we walked their ghosts back to life, resurrecting memories of a world my family had long known. As we neared each familiar place I could feel her memory come back to life in the tightening of her grip on my arm. As I ran my fingers through the dirt my father had plowed and my grandfather had tended, these myths of my past began to come to life. I saw my grandmother walking through the field, Aunt Lula hauling water into the house. I saw Uncle Ben tending a mule, Aunt Ada shelling peas, and my father chopping wood. It opened in front of me like a book, written for me and written about me, that I never experienced for myself.

Slowly, not out of deference to my own will, I began to feel, step by step, the burden passed on to me. I began to feel the sacrifice my grandmother had made—that they all had made—and I began to sense, for the first time, all the ambition and all the risk it took to leave behind the only life they knew and start three hundred miles north, for the *chance* at creating something better. For the chance of something better for *me*.

Being there, with my shoes dusted by the very dirt that bore my history, my past was inescapable. I had not come here to face it, but all around me, in loblolly pines that arched over red cracked clay and crumbling walls vined with ivy, it faced me back. I owned it all. I couldn't simply ignore it any more than I could ignore my own voice. I was within it; it was part of me. What had these trees seen? How could one woman bear this family and this responsibility? The trip had started as a burden, but it was impossible now for me to look at the history around me and feel anything other than stunned, grateful, and a sense of pride for a people, my people, who bore their burdens in the heat of the day and *still overcame*. Too many people had sacrificed too much for me to waste my life. I stood there, alongside my father and his big sister, fifty years after they had left it, and surveyed a past we all bore. I had never felt so connected to her. It was *real*. It had always been real.

For the first time, all the years that led up to my existence breathed with a vibrant sense of life. And as I began to reckon with them I became aware of everything we were with, but also everything we were without. Some ghosts never came back to life

* * *

My trip to Alabama as an adult solidified the connection between the life I would live and the lives around me that had already been lived. More importantly, it revealed layers of my grandmother's story I never completely understood until I stood on the same soil at this point in my life. It was a trip I should have made years earlier. A trip I wish I could have taken with her so we could walk her ghosts back to life, arm in arm, and feel the same breeze and toe the same dirt. But it wasn't until I looked back on the trip years later that I realized she *had* been there, in the dry crabgrass and the cloud of blackbirds. In the honeysuckle and the brittle timbre of Aunt Ada's voice. She was the backdrop we all lived our lives on. She was the anchor of an entire lineage and the first author of hope in my life, all because of a courageous decision she made in a Nashville hospital as a sixty-five-year-old widow unaware of how she was about to change a little girl's world.

* * *

I didn't know who my mother was until I was nine. She couldn't keep me and when she found out her baby-to-be was two for the price of one; she couldn't keep my twin brother Shawn either. The day we were born was the last time I was in the same room as my mother until I was sixteen. She already had four children under ten years old and there was no room for Shawn and me in her equation. She was married and my father engaged with another daughter of his own. And so it was that on the day in 1972 Shawn and I were born we were a simple two-mouth addition onto a scene that already had five mouths to feed. It was too crowded for a pair of unplanned babies to fit in. There was no place for us among them.

Had it been up to my mother's husband, we would not have born at all. He encouraged her to take the easier route for all of them and terminate the pregnancy before it was too late, but she refused. She would bear us for nine months and nothing more. On the day we were born we were brought into the world and then left to it, unclaimed.

My father tried unsuccessfully to convince several family members to adopt us. But taking on a baby that isn't yours is a hard sell for people already struggling. To take on two would be almost impossible. Person after person passed on us, unable or simply unwilling to assume a burden they didn't have to. Out of options and unwilling to accept the responsibility himself, there was one person left in his life he could ask—the last person he wanted to tell about two little babies that now held her last name.

I don't know what was said in the conversation between my father and my grandmother. I don't know how he convinced her, a few years widowed and struggling to make her own ends meet, to visit Nashville General Hospital and lay eyes on two babies she didn't know. I don't know if she got angry with him, or if she didn't believe him, or what circumstances went into her decision to leave her house on Arthur Avenue that day in 1972 and pay a visit to a hospital. I'll never know. All I know is, for whatever reason, she did.

He didn't tell her then the babies were her grandchildren. But I don't think he had to. I also don't think it would have mattered. I saw over the next twenty years a sense of mercy and responsibility in my grandmother that enables me to picture what happened next so vividly, even though I was only days old.

I see Olivia Witherspoon walk in the hospital and look through the glass at the two little bodies unclaimed and alone. Maybe she sees her eyes; maybe she sees her son's nose. Maybe she hears us cry and is taken back to the day in 1927, just twenty years old, when Aunt Lula first pierced her world and her heart. Whatever it was, she sees enough, and then I see her put us in her purse and walk us home. By the way, she actually does put us in her purse and journeys home.

The thing that strikes me most today about grandmomma's decision to adopt my brother and me is her complete disregard for whether her circumstances would allow it. She never paused to consider the convenience, never took a week to get her affairs in order and baby-proof her house, never wondered what her friends or relatives would think of the lunacy of a sixty-five-year-old widow living on social security becoming the guardian of two little babies. And I thank God she didn't. Everything in her life would have told her to leave the problem to someone else. She could have let the state assume us, or left us to a foster home, and she would have been completely justified. How hard was it already to survive on the $180 per month she got in social security? And to stretch that for two little babies, who would quickly become two little toddlers, two little children, two little *teenagers*? Her friends would have understood. Her family would have treated her the same. She had every right to walk out of that hospital, shake her head, and catch a city bus back to Arthur Avenue and say, "Those poor, poor little babies." And I thank God she didn't.

Olivia Witherspoon acted on her heart. She acted out of righteousness and out of justice, because the sixty-five years she spent trying to survive on plantations and in derelict homes were spent proving one thing: a fair chance at life should never be a privilege. Plantation life was never good enough for her family, which is why she stayed behind until Lula and Ada and Ben and James came out of the other side of the Great Depression and made their way one by one to Tennessee, so she could push them and encourage them and know that their perseverance would allow for a day where they would not have to set foot back on plantation dirt until *their* terms dictated it—a day when they could walk arm in arm and know they had found more. I know when she locked eyes with those two babies her heart soared with that same sense of justice and no circumstance would prevent her from doing what was right by God and by her. She could leave us behind no more than she could leave behind her own shadow. She had lived her life to that point so her children could have their day of triumph. She would live her last twenty years so her grandchildren would, too.

That's not to say we wouldn't claw and struggle and live on prayer and six dollars a day in the 70s and

80s to make it. The burden of assuming care for two babies would assure that the last two decades of my grandmother's life would be dirt-floor poor, and that she would spend her final years in the same circumstances she spent her first years, measuring decisions over what couldn't be bought, shopping only with her eyes, marking out her days in coins. In the face of injustice my grandmother had an almost inhuman ability to weigh the cost against her own circumstances. When faced with the reality that her life would get very, very difficult, simply look that cost in the face, raise her chin, and say, "So be it." I learned an early love for the idea of resurrection growing up with grandmomma, because I saw it all around me—cereal boxes resurrected as paper, shirts and blouses resurrected in quilts. Nothing ever truly died at my grandmother's house. Everything had another use. Everything was a patch for something else.

It wasn't easy for a child to understand why the dark clouds that sent kids on our street scampering home would send grandmomma scampering for buckets so that we could catch rainwater to flush our toilet. It didn't make sense that something that fell free out of the sky didn't fall free out of the sink, but she was always there to offer a stinging reminder each time the water bill topped ten dollars. The state of Tennessee valued her years as a mental hospital nurse at less than $2,000 per year in retirement pay. We were going to get a long education in resurrection.

And yet my grandmother made an incredible decision early on—to commit fully, way beyond what was necessary, to being an involved parent in our lives. There was never a moment I lived with her she wasn't there for me. I grew up one block away from a community center where boys and girls my age spent their afternoons away from their moms and dads, or maybe like me didn't even *know* their moms and dads, under the care of volunteers and community leaders who could step in, and I never saw the other side of the community center's front door. I was never allowed to go there because my grandmother controlled my peer influence and gave her life to parenting and caring for us from morning to night. She believed parental involvement was everything, whether that parent was sixteen or sixty-five. She went to every parent-teacher conference, every PTA meeting, every concert and ballgame. She was never just a roof over our heads or a signature on our report cards. She loved in deeds and in sacrifice. She loved by keeping her word.

One of the great gifts she gave was the willingness to invest in my dreams, even if I didn't even know if I wanted her to. When she saw me tinkering on a piano at nine years old she didn't ask me to stop; she asked me if I wanted to learn. And when I said yes, she never said that a woman who couldn't afford to flush her own toilet with city water couldn't afford a luxury like piano lessons. She simply marked out the coins and the day she marked out three dollars' worth I put on an outfit that would one day be a quilt, and we walked three miles to a home in north Nashville that served as a piano studio.

As I grew I began to gain a sense of our poverty. My brother and I were awkward at school, outcasts in every conversation about Christmas lists and birthday presents. I became more of a misfit every year. I measured my thrift store hand-me-downs against the new dresses and blouses of my classmates. We didn't have tons of friends. In our home, vacations were mythical. I never experienced one. I heard about them and saw them on television. Christmas gifts were impossible. I soon began to see the things my grandmother did—the knitting, the recycling, the gardening—not as hobbies or ways to pass the time, but as vital pieces of our survival.

There were times during my teenage years I was ashamed of it. While my grandmother leaned on her own self-dependence to fill in the gaps social security left behind, I asked my high school volleyball coach to drop me off three doors down from our house. I didn't want others to know the truth; I didn't want people to know me as another poor black girl who cut her own hair and whose transient father drifted in and out of her life in the middle of the night. I only wanted to hide it all.

Every Friday night, we would walk to the store together or catch a ride from my father or Aunt Ada and grandmomma would buy the same assortment of groceries each week: flour, cornmeal, sugar, slab of bacon, eggs, and sometimes milk and a dinner meat like a whole hen. Everything else came from her garden. We grew everything else we ate. Olivia Witherspoon's garden burst with life like no other on our street. She tended to it with all the wisdom and care a former sharecropping woman of the early 1900s would provide. Each year it was a picture of bounty against the lean backdrop of our lives. The only way my grandmother knew to go through life was to rely directly upon the earth for survival. What we ate depended on the rain and the heat and the bugs. We learned to hate blossom-end rot on tomatoes and blackberry winters that killed off early strawberries. We ate well in harvest months; we struggled to fill up plates in winter. I would never recognize it, but the garden offered me a precious gift: a symbiotic relationship with all those who came before me. I *did* have a connection to my family's history, even if I never saw it. The earth, as it did for the sharecroppers and laborers before me, was keeping me alive.

My grandmother's garden was the first picture of social justice I ever saw. Arthur Avenue was a collection of Nashville's struggling and hurting people—people often in many of the same circumstances as us. We lived next door to a drunk who often stumbled home badly beaten and hungry, always a day away from sobering up, always a day from getting himself in order. He was a broken man, left to the world much like we had been, with just one source of hope. In harvest months my grandmother, in the midst of our struggle, willingly opened our garden to feed him.

As his neighbor she assumed a part in his survival. The garden became his as it was ours. In winter, with the crop bare, he would appear on our porch hungry, and I remember peeking out the window as my grandmother, with all the right in the world to turn him away, sternly instructed him to sit down and sober up his mouth as she disappeared inside. In the kitchen I would watch her scrape together the remaining flour, cornmeal, bacon grease, baking powder, and milk we had, and then deliver him a skillet of hot cornbread to warm his stomach. I can't imagine she always knew what our next meal would be. I can't imagine it mattered.

Her greatness was always unreciprocated. She never got a thank-you card from the man next door, never a bouquet of flowers for her kindness. Her reward was life, played out day after day through her belief that every person deserved a fair shot, whether that meant twenty years of adoption or a small skillet of cornbread. The abandoned twins at the hospital were her babies, but they had no more right to her last cup of flour than the vulgar drunk who crashed next door. She cared about people, that was all. She took bullets. On the days I would watch our neighbor stumble off our porch full on cornbread; I would often turn behind me and watch grandmomma, without a word, crumble leftover pieces into a bowl of sour milk and mash it together with a spoon. It was the ultimate symbol of selflessness: a home filled with all the soul-satisfying aroma of cornbread, which never settled in the kitchen, but rose out of the oven and drifted right out the front door.

My grandmother's desire to devote herself to giving us the best life she could underscored a critical lesson I carried with me into adulthood: when you commit to providing a better life for someone else—even in small, everyday ways—it raises the stakes of your own life, too. It makes *you* want to be better.

She was paving the roads that would lead us to a better life; living under the same roof, it was only natural she would walk them, too. The day at seventy years old she signed up for her first adult education class so that she could learn to read us the Bible marked a critical shift in her own story. We learned to read alongside each other, sixty-five years apart, each perfecting our silent G's and long E's through a worn copy of Ecclesiastes she could now, finally, read between Sundays. But even that wasn't enough. From there we were expected to memorize the books of the Bible, and to scrawl out verses on the backs of resurrected cereal boxes. We could read now. Our excuses were beginning to drop away. Forty years after she had done the same for her own children, our road to higher education—to our own way out—had been paved.

My grandmother lived most of her life in poverty, but she never let it touch her expectations. Our standards were higher than any of the other kids on our street. She pushed us to be better harder than anyone I ever met, because she knew that's what it would take to break the bonds of Arthur Avenue, to break the bonds of poverty, and to free us to be the best God intended for us. She wanted more for her babies, and she knew she was the only one who could make us want it, too. My father was transient, my mother was nonexistent. It would be up to her if Dawn and Shawn Witherspoon were going to make it off the *plantation* and return only on their own terms.

If we were going to be good, she would have to be even better—and if we were going to read, she would have to learn. If we were forbidden from cussing and drinking, she would treat them as traits of the devil himself. She walked to and from Mt. Bethel Church every Sunday morning with a cane and never had to use it. No one on Arthur Avenue dreamed of disrespecting her.

In a life filled with wanting, these high standards ensured that even if there would always be things we had to do without, we would always have some of the things we needed. We didn't have the latest TV, but we had work ethic. She couldn't buy me a car, but she still gave me drive. She couldn't afford to buy us new clothes or shoes, but she ensured that I had a solid biblical and Christian foundation that would afford me much more than fancy clothes. We would die before we slacked off at home. I didn't see it then, but she was filling the gaps left by the things we couldn't have with all the things we could. By ignoring the superfluous things in life she was teaching us what really mattered. I could never understand how valuable this was. I could never know how these gifts were so much more than a Christmas or birthday present could ever be.

It was only through her investment that we could make it through school. The odds were always against it. But despite the numbers of my classmates who fell off along the way, despite what usually happens to inner-city kids in public school, we thrived there. I loved school and was always great at it, and I found passions there I was encouraged to care about. Without extraneous distractions at home I excelled through high school and success came with hard work and yet a sense of ease because of my natural prowess. I never thought anything of it because it all just seemed to come naturally. It wouldn't be until years later that I would realize just how much work it took to make it seem that way. I couldn't know what statistics she had helped us overcome.

I prayed grandmomma would live long enough to see me graduate from high school. I was never sure if she would. I wanted her to see how her kindness had affected real change. I wanted her, finally, to receive some sort of payoff. I wanted her to know the late nights and early mornings and insane decision to take on a little girl when she was sixty-five years old had been worth it, because in the face of injustice that little girl had looked reality in the face, and like her grandmother, had accepted that sometimes life would get very, very difficult, and simply raised her chin and said, "So be it." I wanted her to be proud of something more than a bucket of rainwater.

In May 1990, my grandmother sat in a large arena for the McGavock Comprehensive High School graduation and watched, for the first time in more than fifty years, a baby reared under her care walk a stage and take hold of a diploma. She was eighty-three years old. She could read. She could live on clabbered milk and bacon grease. She could feed a drunk on a skillet of cornbread. She could see her reward, and if she didn't know what it meant for a black girl from the wrong side of the tracks in Nashville to graduate with a 3.8 GPA and an offer to attend Vanderbilt University, I finally did. I received a faculty award on stage that day and when my teacher gave it to me the only thing I knew to do was to walk right off the stage and hand it to the only woman in the crowd who deserved recognition—the only woman who could carry a cane and know she wouldn't need it.

I left Arthur Avenue for the last time that year. I held offers to attend universities around the country but turned them down to attend a historically black college. I didn't want to be a smart black kid; I just wanted to be a smart kid. I enrolled at Tennessee State University, far enough from Arthur Avenue to have beaten it, but close enough to hold her close to my life.

As she had done for two little girls and two little boys fifty years earlier, my grandmother stayed behind, to push me and encourage me from home. On the day I left for college I was full of the things she had left me with: a sense of purpose, a drive to succeed, a dream to never come back until my terms dictated it. Eighteen years earlier I had been brought to a dilapidated house in the purse of a woman who had decided to devote her last years on earth to providing two little babies a shot. I was leaving it as a woman who knew what love and sacrifice and poverty looked like. I was leaving it as a woman who knew what heartbreak looked like, because she saw it in the eyes of her grandmother when she told her she had broken the reed of her clarinet, and it looked like a woman who knew a seventy-five-cent replacement wasn't possible. I knew what reality looked like. I knew what shame looked like, because it looked like the one clarinet player at McGavock High School who marched with broken reeds, hiding one more burden from her grandmother.

I knew what courage looked like: it looked like sticking your finger in the chest of a violent drunk and telling him to sober up his mouth if he wanted anything to eat. And I knew that compassion looked like a bowl of clabbered milk in an empty kitchen. I knew what it meant to hate something so much the hatred turned to desire, and so I learned to hate being poor and being awkward and going without so that I could turn it into a desire to beat it all and leave it behind me. And I knew what love looked like. It looked like an old woman who watched her last baby leave Arthur Avenue for college and turned back inside to stay behind.

I don't often like to think how my life would have turned out had my grandmother not made the decision she did that day in 1972. It wouldn't do anything for me. How would my life have turned out had she not met my grandfather in 1923, or had my mother and father not met in 1971? What would have happened if my mother had agreed to take us on in 1972? In the end, they're just numbers. Hypotheticals. Myths. Our lives are made up of so many of these numbers—millions of little moments that have to align in just the right way so things play out how they're supposed to. But life is what it is.

There is one number I'm left with, though. When you get to the point in life where perspective offers a chance to look back at the things that built you up, you see something interesting: that past, the random minutiae and innumerable coincidences that made themselves manifest in you, there are some very real, very impactful numbers left behind. Numbers that you wear on your heart as markers—as moments that serve to show you, even years later that hope can be born any day.

Each number we hold is unique to our own lives—a souvenir of survival, a testimony of faith. We all have it: the moment in 1995 the doctor looked up from a clear CT scan, and after years of struggle opened his arms and said, "You beat it." The morning in 2000, when your baby boy first opened his eyes and locked onto yours. The day in 2007 you walked the stage and took hold of a diploma, when no one with your last name had taken the walk before. The day in 2009 you did it again.

To own this number is to own a chance to pass it on. It's knowing that when everyone else sees a few simple digits, you see hope, and it's about birthing that hope in others. That spells the difference in being a person and being a Number Person.

When it came time for me to shake off all the numbers I was leaving behind and embrace the one I would carry with me, only one number made sense. I was already wearing it on my heart. It was a number that represented what greatness really meant—not that it comes in volume or reward, but in the simple, honest, selfless, God-honoring decisions that change the world. And one day I will stand in the dirt of a sprawling plantation in south Alabama and tell my children what 1907 means. I will tell them so that they will feel the burden of a woman who survived bigotry and poverty and only bathed when God saw fit to empty the clouds. I will tell them of a woman who made it through droughts and Depressions and the death of a husband—who survived all of it and still knew she was too good to die not knowing how to read. I will tell them of the richest woman I ever knew.

Two

A Chariot Swung Low

When you become a Number Person the way you see yourself changes. You become beholden to someone else's trust. You become indebted to their belief. When you view your days on earth as a life spun out from a number someone else birthed inside you, that person who made the investment assumes a different role in your life. I always believed in life beyond Arthur Avenue, but that would only get me so far. It was my *grandmother's* belief that actually pushed me out the door, because it drove her to set standards and expectations I could only meet if I pushed myself to accomplish something. My accomplishments grew out of that. And once that began to happen, she knew I was already on my way.

I lived eighteen years on the other side of that dynamic—as a recipient of that trust and belief. But once I had kids of my own I began to understand what it took for her to make that investment. It takes so much faith to push your child to be better than average. It takes so much trust. Every day she made deposits in my life—deposits of encouragement, empowerment, will, effort, and, of course, love. For me to not live up to those investments meant not just failing myself, but failing her, too. When you see your life this way the stakes grow exponentially. You aren't living for yourself anymore. You're living to honor someone else, to carry two people's legacies. You begin to feel the eyes on you. But I have also found that's when your world really comes alive.

I left Arthur Avenue with a sense of purpose. More importantly, I left with a number that had helped me develop one—a number that I could hold on to for the rest of my life that would outlast my own energy and good intentions. From then on, when I saw "1907," I would know that it meant a lifelong belief that I could be more than I thought I could. That I could *do* more than I thought I could. The value in the numbers we hold comes not just in what they mean to us, but that they'll always mean something to us, even when we lose sight of our goals and good intentions. That's the power of being a Number Person. These numbers are gifts because they aren't born out of fleeting moments of inspiration or energy—they are anchored to us by their permanence.

The idea that everyone has a number we carry with us through life is certainly not a new one. Think of what 1944 must mean to a man who was on the beach in Normandy, or what 1969 means to a little boy who watched on a black-and-white TV as someone who used to be a little boy himself stepped out of a spaceship and took the mystery out of the moon. Some numbers have universal impact, and we know exactly what they mean when we see them, and in a matter of hours a Tuesday morning can turn three seemingly innocuous numbers into 9/11.

Numbers gain power in their associations. They recall powerful emotions the same way a passing whiff of cologne brings your father back to life, or the faint rhythm of a familiar song takes you back to that faraway summer night of your first date. Life is all about these associations. Without them it becomes nothing but a line on a sheet of paper, and every day we live gets us one inch closer to the end of the line. Without these associations, what's the sense in living a powerful life? What's the point in sacrifice, or relationships? Without the power of looking backward, our lives become a flat two-dimensional space, running from left to right, and the weight of our actions is undercut by the reality that everything we live for exists only in the moment. Only as a dot on a graphite line pointed in one direction. Their impact doesn't matter, because life is only about the day to come.

Associations—our numbers—change this dynamic. The song that takes you back, the smell that makes you stop, the number that spurs you on—these are the third dimension of life. These are the things that take life off the piece of paper and give it a vibrant sense of connection. These are the things that turn it from a pencil line drawn in one direction into a sphere: a growing, throbbing, interconnected existence that points backward *and* forward, bumping into other spheres and intertwining as it grows, to form a system of conjoined relationships that interact and feed off of each other. That's what life is. That's why we're here. And your number is a major part of that system.

By the time I left Arthur Avenue, 1907 was already imprinted on my heart. That number didn't just define the first eighteen years of my life; it was going to define my entire life, because everything I would do and everything I would strive for would be possible because of it. Unfortunately, as I was about to learn, many times these numbers sit dormant in our lives, and we don't realize the power of their associations until much later. My grandmother spent every day of the eighteen years I lived with her working so that I could have the life I wanted, but the reality was that on many of them she was still knocking against the stubborn brain of a teenager. I walked off Arthur Avenue with an attitude that couldn't understand the impact of 1907, because I was too obstinate to realize it.

When I graduated from high school I desperately wanted to attend Spelman College. A historically black, all-women's school, I wanted to find real relationships there, to live outside Tennessee and chase my own dreams in Atlanta, where I could gain a new perspective and, coincidentally, be in the city where my mother lived. It had everything I wanted in a school, and when my plans fell through, leaving me stuck in Nashville at Tennessee State, I became disappointed and at times stopped trying. I began college with the sense that I was somehow better than that school, rather than filled with gratitude that I was only there because my grandmother had committed eighteen years of her life so that I could be. School had always been easy for me and I thought college would be, too. And after a year I had screwed it up.

I told my grandmother I was quitting school to work, and because of the bone-chilling fear of what would happen if she ever found out I lied to her, I not only did, but I worked three jobs. I deeply wanted and valued an education, and I now saw it as something I had to accomplish. Working multiple jobs would make me feel better about myself. How could someone who graduated in the top 1 percent of her class end up withdrawing from college due to unsatisfactory progress in her first year? I was too proud to admit my failure. I was too proud to admit I might lose the only real ticket I had to changing my life.

Living in Nashville added a peculiar element to the relationship I held with my past. I was gone, in a sense, with my own apartment and own jobs and own concerns, but I wasn't really gone. I wasn't in Atlanta. I was in and out of my old life. I didn't have to be home by dark or let my grandmother know whose house I was going to, but I still spent time there, still called her three times a day, still joined her for meals occasionally, still walked her to church.

I loved walking grandmomma to church. It was a peaceful moment for the two of us to spend together in the quiet of the morning. She was a pillar of Mt. Bethel, a saint within its very walls, and anyone there treated her the way they'd treat God if He came down and sat in the front pew Himself. They fawned over her dresses and her hats, and wanted to know how she was and how Dawn and Shawn were treating her. She'd always just look them back one by one and tell them only as she could do that she was just livin', that God was good to her and that was good enough.

On Sunday, April 19, 1992, as she had done hundreds of Sundays before, she walked along Arthur Avenue in the early morning before the Sunday service. It was four days before my grandmother's eighty-fifth birthday. I still remember with sharp clarity the way the sun crept through the windows that day and warmed her walk to the sanctuary. The associations. You could see how beloved she was to that church in the eyes of every person who gave her a hug and paused to let her pass. She always loved them back, always reciprocated the sense of community.

That Sunday I noticed a peculiar intentionality in the way my grandmother spoke to the people of her church. It wasn't uncommon for her to spin out doorway conversations with the ladies in the church well past closing time, but there was something about her on this particular Sunday that drew me to notice. After the service, I watched her get up and stand in the door of Mt. Bethel, then one by one take in the hands of every single person that walked by her. She drew them close and spoke directly to them. Not a single person left without holding her hand, leaning in close, and sharing a word. She was offering something. I didn't know what.

That Tuesday, two days before her birthday, I crawled up in grandmomma's bed as I had countless times over the years and told her of our plans to come. We wanted to celebrate her, I said. An *eighty-fifth* birthday! But with every detail I offered, she simply replied with a distant, "I don't know." I didn't understand what she was doing, why she would pat me on the hand and say, "We'll see" when I was only trying to give her something to look forward to. It was hard. It wasn't like her. I left her house that day unsure of how I felt and tried to put it out of my mind.

Living with a woman like Olivia Witherspoon, you begin to get a sense of how to treat the world around you. You learn that life is not as much a random scattering of moments as much as it is a narrative that you impact. You learn to fill in the blanks that others leave behind.

You also learn there are times the phone is not supposed to ring. I saw my grandmother the next morning but was away from her that afternoon when the call came, and the moment I heard Aunt Lula's voice on the other end I knew with an arresting sense of clarity that I was about to brush up against one of those moments that splits your life. You need to come home, she told me. You need to be back on Arthur Avenue.

When I arrived in front of the house an ambulance was already on the way. My grandmother was soon strapped to a stretcher and I began to shake. She didn't get carried off that porch; she carried people *off* it with her kindness and her steadfastness and her steaming skillets of cornbread. She didn't get wheeled into ambulances; she marched down Arthur Avenue with a pillbox hat and a cane that told the world she owned the sidewalk and the little house at the end of it.

She looked helpless, not at all like the pillar of a family I knew. My aunt spoke with a fear in her voice that I didn't recognize, and I felt dizzy. My body knew what my mind couldn't handle. I didn't know what was wrong with her or why she had felt sick. I didn't know what the paramedics said or how fast they had rushed there. All I knew was when she watched the ceiling of her house turn to blue sky from a stretcher carried out the front door, the last moment she would spend in our house was over. I knew she would never come back.

As the night wore on we collected at the hospital, as many as forty of us gathered to be near her, to be around her as much as we could just in case there were a fleeting moment she'd call out our name and summon us to her bedside. We wanted to be there in case we heard her call us down the hallway. We wanted to be there in case she needed us as we had needed her. And before long she did. She said she wanted to see her babies.

The doctor said she was speaking out of her mind. But I saw purpose in her eyes and I knew what purpose looked like in the eyes of a woman who had four children but raised six. I knew what intentionality looked like. I knew what Olivia Witherspoon looked like when she had work to do. She gathered Shawn and I to her bedside, took our hands, and pulled us close.

"These are my babies," she told the doctor. "These are my babies. These are my babies."

She wanted him to know. She had things she wanted all of us to know.

"Donna," she said, recalling my old nickname, "I want you to keep serving the Lord and take care of your brother. Shawn, I want you two to take care of each other."

"I will, grandmomma," I told her.

My voice still cowered in the shadow of hers. She was as clear and as focused as I had ever seen her—she knew her work was not yet finished. Every word was intentional. Every word was emphatic. She spoke in declaration, to her babies and to a doctor she wanted so badly to understand. This moment has magnitude, she was telling him. This moment is indelible. These are my babies. This is who we are.

Before long a nurse came in the room and told my grandmother she needed to take three pills. Grandmomma had become very thirsty, unquenchably thirsty almost, and lapped at the water with each pill. After the first, she looked up at the nurse and asked if it was the last one. No, the nurse told her, she still had two to go, and she sat up to take another, then swallowed down a drink and asked again. No, she was told, she still had one more, and she sat up once more, swallowed it down, then settled back, looked out the window, and exhaled. It was another task completed. She was finishing what she started, always seeing things through, down to the third pill washed down her throat.

She spent a long time looking out that window. She was focusing on something we couldn't grasp, longing for something we couldn't see, and I got the sad feeling, just watching her there, that my grandmother was experiencing something we couldn't understand. For the first time I couldn't follow in her shadow. I couldn't walk her by the arm. She was on her own, for the first time leaving us to stay behind, and the window drew a particular focus out of her I did not recognize. I watched my grandmother that afternoon, praying she would make it one more day, make it to April 23, but she died the day before her eighty-fifth birthday.

I stood in the hallway with our family for a long time. We tried to come to an understanding of our loss, but all there was to do was to hold on to each other and weep. Our foundation was gone. Everything we were built on, everything that held us together had left us. What were we standing on? No one could grasp it; we could only shake and cry and clog a narrow hallway of a dimly lit hospital on legs filled with cement. I felt like I was five years old. We all did.

After a while, with my aunts, uncles, and cousins still crying in the hall, I went back inside. Seeing my grandmother gone, I had a vision of someone opening a book in front of me, and I could see every page flipped by, going faster...faster...faster, and then slammed shut. It felt so final. I touched her skin and couldn't feel her inside it. Alone in the room with her, I was back at our table, getting pinned into a dress that didn't fit right, scrambling for a bucket as a shower rolled through, getting told with a firmness that stretched back a generation that there was no need to sleep at a friend's house, because I had a bed, and that bed was good enough. I did a lot of walking in that hospital room. I walked down the street to a piano lesson. I walked to Mt. Bethel. I walked an extra three houses, too ashamed to be dropped off at home. I walked off a graduation stage and into her arms. My history—every record of my life, everything about me—had walked out with her. I couldn't cry with my family. They mourned because they couldn't reckon with how they would go on living. I felt an emptiness that told me I had already died.

The next day, a pastor came to visit. We told him how she went—how she had spent the better part of the day staring out the window at nothing in particular, and how we couldn't understand how she could seem so clear and focused and yet stare so long at nothing. It didn't make sense.

"Ah, but she was staring at something," he said. "She saw her chariot, swung low and ready to take her home."

* * *

By the time I made it back to my apartment that night I had enough life back inside me to turn me to a mess. The only thing I had strength for was to crawl into the fetal position and cry myself in and out of a restless sleep. What in the world would I do? Who was going to take care of me? I wept for seven straight hours out of emptiness, out of anger. I had no parents in my life to watch over me; no relative I would go to take me in. For the first time in nineteen years I was back at Nashville General, abandoned and alone, brought intothe world and then left to it. For the first time in nineteen years, a call for help to Arthur Avenue would go unanswered.

The next day was the lowest point of my life. Her absence was magnified by the celebration that would never be, by the empty chair at the birthday table where we had planned to honor eighty-five years of service and humility. It was going to be a celebration of Olivia Witherspoon's life, and with her so suddenly taken from us, the only thought that occupied our minds was death. The death of our best friend, of our bedrock. The death of our family's legacy. The death of our hope. I had tried to excite my grandmother over the possibilities of Thursday's party, to tell her how we wanted to honor her on her day, and twenty-four hours later she was *gone*. We walked lifeless through the house, swollen with disbelief, through tiny rooms and narrow halls that seemed cavernous without her in them. She had filled them with her presence. She had filled all of us with her presence.

The hours rolled over each other. I drifted in and out of sleep, didn't eat, didn't get out of bed. I was empty and alone and angry. The faith she had instilled so deeply inside me was completely shattered by her absence. How could God take her from me so quickly? How could He do such a thing the day before we were set to honor her life? How could He be so cruel?

Where was the benevolence we sang about at Mt. Bethel? Where was the kind shepherd watching over me? Where was the God who *loved* me? I had been asked, as happened from time to time in those days, to preach a Sunday afternoon service at New Hope Baptist Church on the south side of Nashville in three days. I would stand in a pulpit and read from a Bible that suddenly felt very irrelevant to me. I would expound on the virtues and characteristics of a God who suddenly felt very distant. Would I say things I didn't believe? I would preach with anger in my heart, that God had allowed me to say yes to those people knowing full well that four days earlier my entire life would come unraveled. I couldn't see any sort of bigger picture painted by her death. I couldn't realize that the reason my grandmother couldn't get excited for our party was because she knew a much, much better one awaited her somewhere else.

The next day, the Friday before I was supposed to speak, I had a moment with God. If I was going to stand at the front of that church, it was only going to be after me and Him had it out. I had to know what He wanted from me. I had to know how He expected me to be honest. I was still angry with what He had done, so I needed to know how He expected me to talk to those people. I needed to know what I was supposed to say.

My grief forced me to listen. It forced me to run out of options—out of hope—and really search for something that would honestly help me make it to Sunday. It was a cathartic helplessness, because when I finally heard Him answer, I heard Him say that even if I didn't know what my next nineteen years without my grandmother would look like, or who would pin me into dresses or cast a protective shadow over me, I didn't *have* to know. I didn't have to think about my life without a grandmomma. I just had to get to Sunday. I had to trust Him with my life in the same way my grandmother had entrusted hers and mine to Him years before. One hour at a time, one restless night at a time, I just had to get to Sunday. Somehow, even if it took anger and grief and denial, I just had to get to Sunday. From there, life would roll on; even if I didn't understand how. But Sunday would move me forward. And when I got in that pulpit in two days, the people weren't there to hear from me. They were there to hear from Him.

By Sunday morning I was encouraged not to preach, that there was no way in my condition I would be able to, but I held a vision in my head of a pillar of a woman who never backed out of her word. She held to her principles, this woman, and no matter how empty or angry or lifeless I felt, my last moment alone with her had been spent at the receiving end of a command I would never be able to shake.

"Donna," I heard her say, just hours from death, "I want you to keep serving the Lord."

Our hands clasped tight. I had offered the only thing I had to give. It was the only thing I was ever able to give her. It was the same thing I had given her at six years old, when she saw me ashamed of a patchwork dress and told me to never be afraid of who I was. It was the thing I had given to her at eighteen, when she told me how proud she was of me from the side of a graduation stage, and commanded me to do well with the gift I had been given. And it was the thing I had given to her four days before. I had given her my word.

"I will, grandmomma," I said.

That afternoon, in a three o'clock service on the south side of Nashville, a nineteen-year-old girl from the wrong side of the tracks took the pulpit at New Hope Baptist Church and preached a very specific message on how serving the Lord will reap benefits in your life. It doesn't always happen here, the girl said, and you don't always see the payoff on earth, but there is a By and By where you will. There was a woman in the girl's life who proved it; a woman in her voice who thundered it. A woman in her heart who lived it.

That afternoon, the girl began to find healing. She began to see how God would use a number planted on her heart as a force for good. She began to see how people outlive their days on earth with the greatness they birth in other people. She began to see how good God really is despite pain and hardship. She began to understand God's infinite wisdom and rest in it. She found comfort and peace in the very words from His Word that she shared with others on that day. And when she looked out into the full congregation, through tears that still didn't quite make sense, she realized she had made it to Sunday and found hope there.

The service ended at five. I didn't have time to go home. I had to rush to another appointment. Olivia Witherspoon's funeral was at six.

*   *   *

My message at New Hope had begun my reconciliation with God, as well as the healing process I would have to endure going forward without my grandmother. But in no way was it the solution to the emotional wound that had opened up in her absence. I struggled after she died.

I spent the rest of the spring and summer listless, without the drive and the dream she had birthed inside me. I had lost all my optimism and all the desire that drove me off of Arthur Avenue. All I had was a dirty apartment and a patchwork relationship with God. The idea that the number 1907 meant anything to my life was nonexistent. I fell into depression and filled the hole her absence left in my life with day after day of worthless things and useless friends. I felt wretched.

I had heard very clearly in April God tell me I would get through my grandmother's death because all I had to do was get to Sunday. I didn't have to know what would come after, He had said, or how I would get out of bed on the days I couldn't catch my breath. But I had only taken that promise literally. After that one Sunday message at New Hope, I had spun away a summer I would have never *dreamed* live while my grandmother was alive.

But by the end of the summer I began to realize that the promise I felt from God that day wasn't literal at all. It wasn't Sunday, April 26, that I had to make it to. Sunday didn't begin and end in a twenty-four hour period. Sunday was simply a metaphor for a day when I would have a chance to take action. To honor her by doing what I knew was right, by stepping into a pulpit when I had struggled to still believe in what it meant. And that message *had* begun a healing process. It was critical at getting me through that first week.

If I was going to pull myself out of the spiral I had become caught in, I was going to have to face a few more Sundays. I was going to have to have it out with God again and figure out what it meant to take action. I was going to have to have it out with myself and come to an understanding that I had a responsibility bequeathed to me by Olivia Witherspoon to get back in that pulpit and do what was right. And I was about to get my first chance.

As summer wound down, my friends began, one by one, to go back to school. They were set to begin their junior years and as the fall neared I took inventory of my situation and the three jobs I couldn't break out of and the dirty apartment that hemmed me in and realized that my grandmother did not invest eighteen years in me so that I could quit school after one year. Handling the grief of her death meant making it to Sunday. And that meant sitting down and writing a letter to the Academic Review Board at Tennessee State University.

My pride didn't want me to be honest. My ego didn't want me to admit that I had blown my freshman year and that I wasn't sure if I even deserved a second shot. I was ashamed at what I had done and how I had wasted their belief in me. I wrote the letter. I had made it to another Sunday.

I began college in 1990 with the sense that my academic prowess was all I needed to succeed in college. When I received word in 1992 that I would get a second chance, I lost every notion that somehow being smart was enough. Instead I learned that the life you live is the one you choose. Life isn't fair and it may never be. But we all have a choice in how we respond to it. In the place of intellect, I gained a fire that came with another shot to prove to her, to *really* prove to her, that her investment in me had been worth it. But it wasn't just her. I was about to get another Sunday and it was going to be for my brother who had gone through the fire with me, and for Aunt Lula and Aunt Ada and all the other relatives who built me up—who had prayed for me and shared my name and been so proud of me on the day in high school I was elected president of a national youth conference that they all came together and gathered their money to buy me a decent suit. It was for the people who gave me dignity. Who made me proud to hold my last name. I no longer saw education as a ticket out. It was a ticket *to*. Grandmomma would often say, "It makes no sense to have all of that book sense and no common sense." I finally understood.

Back on campus, I quickly found the fire that was missing my first year of college. I found the tenacity I left behind. For the first time in my life, I lived a passion, in every student loan bill and every can of beans. My scholarships were long gone. It was my turn to count coins and measure out my decisions with crumpled bills. I felt again what it meant to have a dream, because it felt a lot like not being sure if you could find enough quarters to eat a hamburger. It felt like watching my friends earn their degrees, then earn their master's degrees, then leave me two steps behind, struggling to keep my head above water and my lights on. It felt like earning something.

Some days it felt more like a dream than others. Some days a dream is all it felt like, because the reality of actually receiving an education seemed impossible. I knew more than anybody on that campus what it meant to live in poverty, because I had beaten my head against it for nineteen years. And yet, with Arthur Avenue behind me, I still could not claw hard enough to climb out of it. I cried at home, unsure of how I'd pay my water bill. I cried at work, overwhelmed at another schedule that forced me to miss class. And I cried at the registrar's office, faced with another tuition balance that I couldn't afford to pay, another insurmountable $150 hold on my account I knew I had no way of paying. I cried in the car on the way home, unsure if I would ever finish what I had started.

I took classes in the morning and in the afternoon; I took every class I could. I fell in complete love with education, and yet after five years of struggle I still did not have a degree to show for it. Every class I needed had to be squeezed around the jobs I held to make it by, and it was impossible to gain traction. I had gone from an eighteen-year-old advanced placement scholarship student to a twenty-five-year-old college senior, borne back year after year into struggle, feeling like the entire world was leaving me behind.

For six years the only thing I could keep my eyes on was a principle I learned from Olivia Witherspoon—that some people just get an extra dose of adversity in their life, and really it's a blessing, because once you're around it enough you begin to develop the sense that the payoff waiting in the By and By, whenever that will be, is going to be extra sweet. You begin to see adversity as just a precursor to a reward that's on its way. That was the point of the message I had preached six years earlier at New Hope. That's why my grandmother, after eighty-four years and 364 days of struggle, was only looking forward to one birthday party. Her struggle was about to end. I sensed mine would, too. I had made it to

Sunday. I had found a life of Sundays. And I didn't have to be told the story of the prodigal son. I had scrawled it out, years ago, on the back of a cereal box that served as paper.

* * *

Graduation practice for Tennessee State University was held in the school's Gentry Auditorium. We gathered to go over the proceedings, a buzz of excitement and energy, and as we rehearsed there was a moment, somewhere in the haze of the crowd and the commotion, someone sidled up beside me and handed me a clear plastic bag, and my heart flipped inside my chest. I could see the cap and gown inside. Being handed the cap and gown meant your final credits had gone through. It meant the check had cleared. It meant the last strip of red tape had been eviscerated. Standing there, amid the chaos swirling around me, I stared at a flimsy plastic bag with tears running down my cheek.

Memories began to flood back—memories of Arthur Avenue, memories of her and of the life we lived together. I thought of my best friend, and how when she left me six years before, she left me with a debt I would never fully be able to repay. I thought of my brother and my family and of that day in the hospital we laid our heads on each other's shoulders, wondering what we stood on. Wondering how we'd ever make it to a Sunday. I was overwhelmed with her presence, overwhelmed with gratitude that I had been given a second chance, and wished so badly she could have been there.

"I hope I made you proud," was all that I could say.

Later that week I walked my second stage, and the awkward girl from Arthur Avenue, finally, was left on the other side. I had fulfilled my hero's belief in me. I knew, for the first time, what it felt like to be empowered. As I made my way across the stage, I scanned the crowd. I was focusing on something no one else could grasp, longing for something I knew I wouldn't see. There was a woman I wanted to share it with, a woman whose belief in me changed the trajectory of my life. But I could not see her. My heart racing, I climbed down, shaking with the power of possibility.

Three

Perfectly Losers

By the time I graduated from college I had three very real numbers on my heart. The first, 1907, spoke to the woman who birthed hope in my life, who saved me and always believed I was worth more. The second, 1992, would recall the time she left us, but more importantly the time I was forced to assume responsibility of the woman I saw in the mirror. The third, 1998, would remind me of the power of that responsibility, and what I was capable of when I reckoned with my own potential.

I was gathering these numbers like arrows in a quiver, picking them up as I got older and packing them away on my back. With every transcendent moment in my life, I was building a collection of tools to use as I went forward. Life is a journey and you need everything you can use to get through it. There will be days when opening your eyes in the morning is the furthest you think you'll get. On these days, my weapons would be these moments. My tools would be these numbers. When I thought of them—1907, 1992, 1997—it became impossible to be complacent about my day. When I think of them still, they spur me to action. They remind me to hope, because I was hoped in; to work, because I was worked on; and to achieve, because I was worth it. They make life *more*. It's not possible to just get by when I think of these numbers. And that's where their power lies.

If you believe everything in life happens for a reason, then not doing this—not carrying something with you to recall the moments that changed your life—is like going to college and never going to class. It's like going on vacation and never leaving the hotel. These things that happen to you—the tragedy, the hardship, the achievements—they are meant to be remembered. They are given to you as gifts you can use to change the world. Even if it's hard, even if your number recalls pain you thought you buried, there can be great value in carrying it forward in some way. If it forces you to take action, or to take hope, then there is power there.

My numbers did not always bring nice associations. 1907 could remind me of the pain of poverty as much as it did the hope of beating it. My first association with 1992 is grief and loss, and even though 1997 brought with it the glory of finally graduating from college, it could also remind me of how hungry and broke I was during that struggle. But accomplishing great things means looking beyond these first associations. It means digging a little further for a feeling you can turn positive. So for 1907, poverty becomes hope; for 1992, grief becomes independence; for 1997, brokenness becomes achievement.

The painful thing in your past—this moment of grief and loss—you can't change it. You can only change how it affects you. That might mean burying it somewhere deep where you never have to be reminded of it again. Or it might mean turning it into a number that stands for something more. A symbol that goes beyond the pain you felt. A marker that reminds you that life is too short, too immediate, and too valuable to waste. And if you have a past that is too painful to reckon with, today is a great time to start moving forward. Look at the calendar. Look at the clock. Moment by moment, the numbers all around you are unlit sparks waiting to explode.

And now the world has opened up, not as a place where we simply get through life, but as a place where we all have the potential to change it—even those of us who have suffered unimaginable pain and loss. And that's the only reason I can think of a night in an Arizona emergency room in 2004 and feel something beyond the paralyzing grief that night brought: because I had seen grief before and knew the hope, by God's grace, that could grow out of it.

* * *

After graduation I had created an incredible sense of momentum for myself. Following college I wrote for two newspapers, worked in TV broadcasting, and had my own radio show in Nashville. The energy that takes action has such an addictive quality to it. Carrying the momentum I used to finish college into everything that lay beyond it felt so natural. Once I saw I was capable of doing what it took to finish school, I could see the things life held from there. I had found real success in a short amount of time, and my eyes were locked on what was to come. For the first time since she left me I felt I was being true to my grandmother. For the first time I felt I was being true to that number.

Not long after I finished at Tennessee State I had a big job interview for an editing position at the Nashville Baptist Publishing Board. I had considered leaving Nashville to work at the Atlanta Journal-Constitution but took the interview anyway just to see what would happen, and when I walked in the office I was introduced to a woman named Christina. I was a good enough interview back then, polished and sharp enough to make myself presentable, but as the interview carried on I found my mind wandering away from the reason I was there. I had a strange feeling being in the office—the sense, just sitting across the desk from her, that I had met someone who was going to be a major influence in my life. It was bizarre. It was the first time I had felt that.

Shawn and I had grown up with so few friends and so many friends from college had moved on their lives. I had had very few heart-deep relationships with someone outside my family. I had searched many places for one, and surrounded myself with many people I felt would provide it, but had often been left wanting. But I knew sitting across from Christina the spark was there. I knew I had to work with her. Before long I couldn't even remember what I was interviewing for, but I hoped with everything I had in me I would get the job. When I got a call a few weeks later telling me the job was mine, I was elated. Christina and I became fast friends in the two years I edited a newspaper there. In my interview, she would tell me later, she had decided to hire me as soon as I told her about my grandmother.

Though I had worked for several companies out of college, the entrepreneurial spirit I gleaned from my grandmother and father held strong in me, and I was always looking for opportunities to express it. Two years into my tenure at the Publishing Board, a co-worker named Toby approached me with an idea for a side publishing company he wanted to start. Overhead costs in publishing are very high—the capital you need to get started and operations costs associated with regular publishing are significant—and we knew we didn't have the resources to do it. But together we began to massage the idea into something else. Eventually we had an idea to start an Internet design company, which we called GreatBusiness.net. We would buy a website and lease space on it to small businesses for thirty dollars a month while offering add-ons like design services and email addresses. The idea was to lower the barrier for small businesses to market themselves on this new thing called the Internet. The draw of a new field—an entire new industry, really—was captivating, and we began to sketch out the company on the side.

I was head of marketing and sales, Toby was in charge of technology, and I brought on Christina to handle customer care. It was my first real hands-on experience with a start-up of this magnitude, and I quickly became addicted to the energy of it. I invented marketing schemes to grow us, learned to handle back-end coding, and thrived on the 24/7 stamina a start-up requires. I really felt, for the first time, I had found the thing I was meant to do.

We embraced the unknown and welcomed the risk, and prepared to launch the company with a huge introductory launch party. Hundreds of invitations were sent out to Nashville businesses, and we rented a room at a downtown high-rise. One by one, RSVPs came back until they formed stacks, verifying the hunch we already felt that our idea was not only viable, but filled a hole in the market. We were nervous and excited for what it meant. GreatBusiness.net was about to open for business.

On the day of the launch party, Toby, Christina, and I waited in a conference room of the Bellsouth building in Nashville for our clients to show. The morning started quiet, and we shook it off to a slow start. But by the afternoon, the crowds were still missing. The RSVPs we waited for—all the dozens of businesses that told us they were coming—never showed. Hour by hour, the room held empty. Eventually, a few brave business owners showed up for our introductory seminar but none signed up for our services.

None of it made sense. I was head of marketing and I had done everything I could, taken every step I could, and held a stack of cards in my hands that promised me the work had paid off. We had an initial customer base headed our way. They had *told* us they were coming. But longer and longer we stood alone. By the end of the day we had spoken to just ten businesses. For the first time our energy for the company we had started was punctured.

One of the hardest things to do when you're an on-the-side entrepreneur is to put your passion project in your back pocket and return to your full-time job—especially after a failure. You drum up so much energy for a start-up, invest so much work and effort, and then have to pretend it doesn't even *exist* and put on a happy face at your regular job. But the next Monday morning back at the Publishing Board we put our heads down and had to go back to work.

Not many days later, the three of us were called into our boss's office separately one by one. As we sat across from him he confronted us about the company we had started. He knew what we were doing. He knew about the launch party and in shocked silence I realized he was somehow responsible for personally contacting many of our RSVPs and told them not to come.

Then, almost as if he had been building toward it, he finished with a sharp crescendo.

"And you," he said, "are fired."

The start-up world requires skin like rubber. In one swing we were now full-time entrepreneurs, and being bitter about our breakup with the Publishing Board wasn't going to do a thing to help get our feet back under us. When you depend on yourself for success you have to learn what it means to bounce right back to form when things go wrong. Businesses are conditioned to destroy start-ups. New companies challenge the processes that already exist; they scoff at the established order. New businesses essentially tell established companies *they* can do it better. Of course people feel threatened. People will go to incredible lengths to protect their ways of doing things and will do everything they can to challenge you. You have to be built like a rubber band to start something, able to bend right back when someone stretches you thin. You can't survive otherwise.

In that sense, getting fired from the Publishing Board was an incredible gift. Not unlike the death of my grandmother years earlier, it took the training wheels off of my life and forced me to survive on my own. If I was going to make it as a businesswoman I was going to have to really become a great marketer. And with our full-time jobs behind us, GreatBusiness.net really started to grow. This enticing thing called the Internet was beginning to become a real draw for small businesses that wanted a piece of it, even if they didn't fully understand it. Soon we attracted big names like GM and the *Nashville Review* and even some Sony artists. We built websites and email addresses and grew the company for two years—incredible longevity for three fired publishers branching out into the tech world.

But I felt restless. The notion of a start-up was strong inside me, but I didn't yet understand that there are all kinds of "start-ups" around us, and new businesses are only part of it. I know now God wired me to seek "start-ups" in every aspect of my life—new relationships, new scenes, new ingenuity—and I still had a very real heart for publishing. So less than three years into our business, I sold my shares to Toby and Christina and began work for another publishing company, for less money, as a copy editor. My life needed a new start-up. A year later Christina sold her shares and joined me.

GreatBusiness.net carried on without us, and when the final shares were sold off years later we learned how our baby project had grown into a viable business asset that was coveted by other companies. We learned how we had laid the groundwork for something that grew and thrived beyond our influence. And when the final shares of the company were sold off, we learned, with a grimace, how wealthy we would have become had we seen it through.

Thankfully, I was too busy to be worried and focused on God's plans for my life in that moment. My life was completely absorbed with work and church. I was now four years beyond college and a thousand miles from the shy girl who struggled to find her purpose. I felt my life had everything it needed—I certainly had all the purpose I needed from it—and at thirty years old I was confident and sure enough of myself to be able to go through it on my own volition.

Christina was concerned about me finding a husband. She often prayed about it and firmly believed God had instructed her to do so. As she would go throughout her day, she would actively seek out a husband for me. At the grocery store, the bank, at Auto Zone and the pharmacy—no man in Nashville was safe. "I'm praying for a husband for my friend," she would tell others. All around Nashville men were approached out of the blue with the bizarre proposition that they could literally be God's gift to a woman. Needless to say we didn't get many returns.

I would tell Christina that it would take a miracle if I ever did find someone, because he would either have to work with me or go to church with me if we were ever going to meet, and there weren't any men in those circles that fit the bill. She prayed *constantly* that I would find a husband. I did it more rarely, content to wait for God to show me this mythical man, if that man even existed, and otherwise I would let my weird train of a life click along whatever tracks it ran. My heart really yearned more to have children. But I fought back the heartache of that emptiness through the amazing nieces, nephews, and godchildren I had already been given, and was content to parent them as an aunt and godmother.

Part of my job was to travel to conferences around the country, and as a speaker I built something of a national platform for our company. One night in late July 2002, I was teaching at a conference and afterward was invited to take part in a faculty banquet. This happened from time to time, and on this particular night Christina was at my table, sitting near me and an older man named David I happened to know from other conferences. The dinner began uneventfully, but as we tackled the salad course I heard Christina's voice pipe up next to me, and I froze in fear.

"Now listen," she said. I was mortified. I looked at her sharply from across the table. "I'm looking for a husband for my friend Dawn."

I closed my eyes in horror. I wanted to laugh it off as a joke, to tell the table that I didn't even know this strange woman, but as I opened my mouth to speak we were both cut off.

"Huh," I heard someone say. "I'm looking for a wife for a man."

Everyone turned to look at David. At this point my only survival tactic was to play it through as a joke.

I said. "Let's hear his resumé."

To my shock, David took me seriously and began, line by line, to recite his son Michael's life story, from birth to the present. Michael was raised by his missionary parents and was now a semi-conductor engineer in Phoenix for Intel. Everyone stopped eating to listen as David talked up his son's heart, personality, intelligence, and kindness. Egged on by the table, we traded information.

That night I couldn't sleep. When I ran into David the next morning I felt supremely awkward around him. I had known him for almost five years and now couldn't even speak his name. In an odd way, I felt *related* to him. He didn't tell me he had called his wife the night before back in Richmond and told her he had met someone whom he wanted Michael to meet. And he certainly didn't tell me that at that very moment she was telling Michael by phone in Phoenix there was a woman in Tennessee who wanted to meet him.

The conference ended the next day and I had asked to be let out of my teaching in the final sessions. I wanted to come home. Though my schedule had been cleared, I was asked to attend at least one class at the conference before I returned to Nashville. In the class, Chris Jackson, the teacher, offered an illustration. Chris had a volunteer stand in front of the class and put his hand on the person's shoulder. "I'm going to play the role of God," Chris said, and commanded the volunteer to walk in a straight line. As the man walked, Chris whispered "turn right" and "turn left" in his ear, all while keeping his hand on his shoulder, guiding him forward. "This is how it is to hear from God about our purpose," Chris said. "He has His hand on you. And when we hear His voice, we have to make the choice to follow Him even when it seems as if our life is on its straight path. God may have a different plan for our lives at this moment in our lives"

It was the only thing I could think of the rest of the class. To hear so clearly that we have to stay close to the voice of God spoke directly to where I was. True to my nature, I was already looking at my next step. I was enrolled in seminary, working toward a Master's degree, and was already making more money than I ever thought I would in journalism. I had been comfortable where I was. But hearing those words had opened up a place inside me that had never been there. The instant I heard them I felt uncomfortable. For the first time I felt unsettled where I was. For the first time I felt unsettled in Nashville.

On the way out of the conference I passed Christina.

"Don't bother coming to church if you don't call him" she said.

* * *

He picked up after two rings. I spoke right away.

"So what's so wrong with you that your dad has to find you a girlfriend?"

"I could ask you the same thing."

"Perfect," I said. "We are both perfectly losers."

Our first conversation lasted four hours. This was a record for him.

He had a bachelor's degree in physics and a Master's degree in engineering physics. He lived alone in a house in Phoenix and worked in what I thought sounded like a very intriguing job. In those four hours I knew without any doubt this was the man God had planned for me. I didn't feel "in love" with him. I did love him. All I knew was I wanted to commit the rest of my life to him.

Michael, on the other hand, was not ready to commit to anything. At the end of our first conversation, when I was floating on a euphoric sense of happiness and was practically ready to pick out a dress, he asked if I could send him a picture of myself for "visual confirmation." He was, after all, a guy. So a few days later I emailed him a picture of myself and never asked for one in return. What I got back was a huge picture of the Grand Canyon with a tiny figure standing next to it in the distance. I had no idea what he really looked like. But it didn't matter. Everything we said about ourselves complemented the other person. He was reading in his free time the books I was reading in seminary. I had prayed for a husband; he had prepared his house for a wife. In our second conversation, that Tuesday night, Michael asked me to share my salvation testimony with him. He asked me about mission work and if I could see myself living in another part of the world. I was riveted by his mind. Everything I had remotely hoped for, he was.

The following Saturday, seven days after we had first spoken, he performed the ultimate profit-loss analysis on me.

"Hypothetically," he said, "If I asked you to marry me, what would you say?"

We had never said "I love you." We had never seen each other face to face. I still had no idea what he looked like. The only thing I knew about him was he was proud of the Grand Canyon. But he could see my smile through the phone and so I agreed to come see him in Arizona.

When we talked he always sounded like he was smiling. And when I got off the plane, with no real way to identify him, I looked into the crowd of people in the terminal and saw a man, meek and patient, beaming. His mother had told him to wear his nicest Polo shirt. He was in his good jeans. Side by side, he took my arm and walked me out of the airport and into his life.

We ate cheap Chinese food. He showed me his empty house. He had taken care of everything making sure I never had to ask for a thing. It felt like a dream. I didn't *know* this man a month before. But bit by bit I grew confident in him, swept up in the whirlwind of our summer and carried on by the inescapable feeling that we were created for each other.

The same evening I arrived, Michael asked me to take a walk with him. He took me to a nearby park and we held hands, the only people in Arizona. The second we hit the grass the sprinklers cut on, and we shrieked as we ran through them to a dry bench. Mildly wet and heaving with laughter, he asked me to marry him. It was the first time we said "I love you." We had known each other in person for barely one day.

Our whirlwind carried through the holidays. Michael met my family in September, and I spent Thanksgiving with him in Phoenix, then Christmas in Nashville with my family and then in Richmond with his family. Christina and I drove my belongings to his house in January and by the time of our wedding I had set a hard and fast new direction for myself. I bought a one-way ticket from Nashville to Maui, and a one-way ticket from Maui to Phoenix. We were married March 29, 2003, a warm Saturday in the spring, the first free moment we had.

* * *

My first year in Arizona with Michael continued the frenetic rhythm of life I was used to. We hiked and we ran, we traveled to San Diego on weekends and flipped months off the calendar with a joyous sense of life. I missed Nashville and everything I had left behind, but my past was starting to slip two or three steps behind where I was. Arthur Avenue and Tennessee State and GreatBusiness.net felt like whole lifetimes ago. The aspirations I had as a journalist and an entrepreneur and an editor were grabbing at me differently than they had before. My life was consumed with my new husband and the things we discovered about ourselves.

We loved the two-person life we had built for each other. Life just felt easy. Everything was a celebration, everything was something new, and I learned what it meant to find joy in the everyday—in the small moments, like organizing the bookshelf or cleaning out the car. We cherished these small moments and found great contentment in them, which is why on Michael's first birthday that we celebrated together we were doing the most basic thing, laying sod in the yard, happy just to be near each other, when I learned he would be getting an extra birthday present.

We had only been married eleven months; a positive pregnancy test was going to change the fabric of our relationship. But I could not have been more thrilled. God had confirmed my every prayer. This baby would be a wish fulfilled.

We learned I was pregnant March 1, four weeks before our first anniversary. We decided to celebrate out of town and booked a trip to Flagstaff, where we would mark our first year with total anticipation of the joy to come.

I fell completely in love with the idea of being pregnant. I subscribed to every magazine, read every book I could find, and marked off the days that would lead us to November. I stayed active. This was different than graduation or launching a new business—for the three decades I lived without a partner, the void I felt to have a child was not possible. It was an unbridgeable gap that I chose not to cross until I met Michael. And I ached for a child. Michael's birthday changed everything.

We bought baby stuff. We began to associate ourselves as a family of three instead of a marriage of two. Our anniversary trip to Flagstaff was the celebration of a year together, but also one of the only chances we would get to celebrate a life-changing moment as just the two of us. And we were going to have a good time doing it.

We were playing pool that Friday afternoon in a restaurant. It was a bit chilly in Flagstaff and we felt close to each other. The year had gone fast. It was joyful to have an anniversary and Michael and I had spent the entire weekend together celebrating the end of our first year. It was amazing how things had changed for us. A year earlier he was an Arizona bachelor with a bare-walled house. I was a single woman whose best friend tried to get her dates at Auto Zone. Thank God we had found each other.

My pregnancy to that point had been uneventful. It was still early and there were many months ahead of belly bulging and late-night cravings. In many ways my body didn't yet *feel* pregnant. So we did things like travel, spend long afternoons at local bookstores browsing the newest non-fiction releases, or playing pool at a restaurant. It was normal for us to be out. And that afternoon, like any other, we were out after a late lunch when I felt the first twinge of pain I didn't know.

At first I tried to put it out of my mind. It could have been heartburn or a cramp or any of a hundred things, so I told Michael not to worry. But the pain worsened by the hour and was impossible to ignore. Soon I began to bleed, and by the time we rushed to the hospital I was in extreme pain.

I had not slept well the night before. I didn't often dream about the baby, but that night I could vividly see our child trying to speak to me, and I could not talk back. We felt far from each other, as if we could reach out but never touch, and it left me empty and confused.

Since I had learned of the pregnancy I had prayed constantly for our child, and felt with every prayer a brick had been laid in the foundation of our relationship. I was giving our child *life*. I spoke to our child and sang to our child and as a first-time mother I spent entire days thinking of the joy we would have together. But that dream rattled me. It was the first time I felt something sever that connection, and I woke up feeling uneasy about it. I hadn't mentioned the dream to Michael.

In the emergency room later that afternoon, the doctor performed an ultrasound and didn't tell us much. I was only a few months on, so he said to take it easy and sent us home. But the joy of our time together had been punctured. We were left with questions. The doctor told us to go on with the rest of our trip, but we didn't feel much like celebrating. We decided to spend the night and head home the next morning.

We arrived back at our hotel in an hour and the moment I walked through the door I felt dizzy and began to severely bleed. My vision went black and within minutes I was slipping in and out of consciousness. I couldn't stand. In panic, Michael helped his bleeding wife out of the hotel bathroom and rushed us to the nearby hospital once again.

I look back on my life now and I see indicators—little moments of prescience that come before certain events that are given to prepare me for what's to come. I see little moments God knew I would need, to ready me for a time I wouldn't understand. Months earlier, on one of our first Sundays together at our church in Phoenix, Michael and I attended a married couples Sunday School class studying the marriage vows, and what "for better or for worse" meant in a marriage. It opened a great conversation between Michael and me, one that we had not had before. What would "for worse" look like for us?

Our time together had been such a whirlwind, it was impossible to plan for every contingency. Michael was so analytically minded and prone to preparation. We had prepared for each other for years, but once our lives intersected it was a rush to live them together. Much of the time we would spend getting to know each other would have to come after we exchanged vows; much of what we learned about each other would be after we were already living together. Sundays like the one that got us talking were invaluable to help this process. They opened conversations we never considered we'd need. They prepared us for things we might endure.

Back in the examination room we met again with the doctor. He examined me and spoke carefully about what he saw.

"Earlier when we performed the ultrasound," the doctor said, "the baby's development did not match up with where you said you are in your pregnancy."

Something dropped inside me.

"Mrs Cornelius, your baby has no heartbeat. The baby has died."

The room was silent. I counted the buttons on the ultrasound machine. My chart hung on the door. So we had already lost him before Flagstaff. At dinner and during dessert, at the pool table before the hemorrhage, he was already gone. Maybe during my very prayers for him his development had already been arrested and I was praying for a life that could never be. The pain and the bleeding were just loud announcements of his exit from our world. I suddenly felt very empty and became conscious of the void inside me. The tears began to roll down my cheeks and the crying became uncontrollable as we held each other grieving the child we would never meet. Michael cried, helplessly held me close and eventually slowly pushed me in a wheelchair from the hospital, the tomb of our grief, and then we left the hospital and drove the hour back in heartbreak and silence.

* * *

My grandmother's death had been the hardest thing to endure before Flagstaff, but the pain and loss that came with losing our child was horrendous.

Nothing could compare to it. Even the word, *miscarriage*, seemed so clinical and detached. It didn't seem to be about the child I had carried. It didn't seem to be about the two of us.

These indicators we are given, these things sent to prepare us, are not often realized until after we use them. We did not think, during this horrible time, how that Sunday in Phoenix had gotten us talking, or forced us to consider what "for better or worse" meant for us. But its power and purpose was undeniable. Because that Sunday Bible study, the one we attended before I even knew I was pregnant had been about the biblical story of Hannah, and the death of her baby. It had been about the most unimaginable loss. It had been about a mother who felt a life ripped away from her.

On the way home from church that Sunday, Michael's brain mulled over what we had heard.

"If something like that that ever happened," he said, "what would I need to do?"

We talked out the exact scenario. I told him what I would need, and what I guessed it would feel like. We talked out how people would treat us, and how it might feel to go back to being just the two of us. When the moment actually happened, our lives fell into the protocol we had already established. What I told Michael months earlier was to protect me. And so he did. He answered the phone and kept his hand on my back in public. He sheltered me from having to tell the story and having to share my feelings. He offered himself in my place. He offered his own vulnerability to keep me safe, knowing all the while there was no one there to protect him.

When we arrived back home in Phoenix, our house was littered with the baby's things. Piles of baby magazines and newborn toys stared us back. In every corner of our house we were haunted by the groundwork that had been laid for memories that would never be. In every corner I saw the things we were with paint a picture of what we would be without. There was nowhere to go to escape it. Our entire house, prepared to be a home to cradle a new life, was an empty shrine to a life we would never meet. We were emotional zombies for weeks.

I bled profusely in the days after the hospital and we prayed I would stay healthy. Michael sought counsel from our pastor and his advice had been to try to establish some sort of normal routine back in our lives. So Michael went back to work. It was hard for him to leave my side. He checked on me constantly, but we felt that carrying on, even if it was hard, was the right first step to take to re-establish our lives. But I fell into a deep depression. I felt broken and vulnerable and told people how I was hurting. There was no way for them to relate. I was a mother without proof. I didn't feel like I had miscarried; I wasn't even sure what that word was supposed to mean. I had lost a child, but nobody could tell me that.

Hope would not come easy. Soon after we returned home it was Mother's Day, and our church held a celebration to honor the mothers in the congregation. I wanted to go, to show I could be strong and that we still held hope in our loss, but as we sat near the front of the sanctuary that morning, surrounded by beaming mothers, I felt my chest tighten and my throat swell.

"Today," our pastor began, "we want to celebrate mothers..."

Why had we even come? What good could possibly come of it? I felt the eyes of the entire sanctuary boring into the back of my head. Being absent from their joy was torturous.

And then our pastor did something that changed the trajectory of my grief. As he prefaced his message on the love of a mother, he turned and looked straight into my eyes. "We want to celebrate mothers," he said, "who have their children, and mothers who do not."

Later, as we sought healing, a family pastor in the church confirmed to us the truth we so needed to hear: We had not simply miscarried. We had lost a child. A real, vibrant, living, developing child. These moments were the first times someone had affirmed it to us. The hurt that was real, the brokenness we felt—those were all there because part of us no longer was. I *was* a mother. I had cared for a child and lost it. I was grieving as a mother should.

Soon after, a friend suggested that we name our child. We hadn't thought in our grief that delving further into this person we lost would help, and so there was still a kind of disconnect to a baby we never fully got to know. We didn't even know if our child was going to be a boy or a girl. But giving the child a name would strengthen our connection, we were told. It would give us a stepping stone for our grief, because it would make real the person we were grieving.

I have always found great significance in rivers. Rivers carry people; they carve away land and give life to the world they come in contact with. Rivers divide cities and villages and transform communities. There is great symbolism in rivers, and in crossing rivers. There was great significance for the people of Israel when they crossed the Jordan River. It meant they would start a new life. It meant entering a place of hope.

When we lost Jordan, we lost a very real part of who we were. The joy that awaited us was stolen away. But there was great significance in our loss. Rivers create life, even in what they carve away. We don't know if Jordan was a boy or if she was a girl. We won't meet Jordan here. But I know of a day I find hope in thinking of when we will reach out to each other and finally touch. We won't feel far from each other on that day. The grief and loss we felt will finally be gone, and a part of me that's been missing since that April night will be returned. We will be swollen with love and reunited forever. We only have a river to cross to get there. A Jordan River.

* * *

I didn't want to get pregnant again. I didn't feel like I could endure the emotions of it, to come to know another child, Jordan's brother or sister, and for nine months be reminded of our loss when I saw myself in the mirror. I was scared. But God has His own ways of bringing healing. And when I found out in September that we would be doing it all over again, I spent every second of the fall and winter afraid of what it might mean.

It's common for mothers who endure miscarriages to suffer their own blame. It's your body, your womb. And when something in your body goes wrong you see yourself as a broken woman—a woman whose body was not good enough to bring her own child to life. I suffered this guilt, as many women have. Beyond it, however, I found it so much harder to forgive myself because of the way I had acted when I first learned I was pregnant: I wanted to prove a baby inside me wouldn't hinder my active lifestyle. So I ran my usual forty miles a week. I hiked. I was so active with Jordan because I wanted to prove how active a pregnant woman could be and so afterward I blamed myself for what happened. I blamed myself, because I thought I might have been the reason we lost Jordan. I couldn't let it go.

So when I became pregnant a second time, I decided on another approach: I would do *nothing*. I was going to save this child. So I barely got off the couch. I spent almost the entire pregnancy too scared to move, or to travel, or to be active at all. I gained significant weight. The grief from Jordan's death kept me grounded. It chained my feet to the ground. The emotions surrounding what happened were still so fresh and raw, I couldn't reckon with how going through it all over again was making me feel. But the thing about being pregnant is that once you *are* pregnant, you really don't have much choice but to just *be* pregnant. And so, less than five months after our first pregnancy, we would endure it all once again.

As it had with Jordan, the first month of my second pregnancy played out with no issues. I slept it away on the couch and prayed the fall and winter would tick by and we could make it to the spring in one piece. I felt relatively fine. But I knew that didn't count for much.

A month or so into the pregnancy I was at a routine wellness visit when the doctor pulled me aside. I had not felt anything too out of the ordinary to that point. My heart dropped.

"Dawn," the doctor said, "we need to speak to you about something."

I swallowed hard. Images of another hospital room began to flood back. I couldn't think. Just a few months in was the point we had lost Jordan. Just a few months in, with everything feeling normal, this was the point he had left us. My throat tightened.

"Dawn, there's no issue with the baby," the doctor said. "But earlier on one of your scans we noticed something that we need to take a look at."

I froze.

"Looking over your scan, I saw a lump on your breast."

My eyes locked onto the doctor. "If this is cancer, you can do chemo in the second trimester and it won't affect the baby. That's your call," he said. "But Dawn we're pretty sure of what we saw and there is a possibility that you could have breast cancer."

A very real part of me froze in fear. But another part of me kicked in—a part I had not felt in a while. I felt the immediate need to act. I rushed to talk with Michael and told him that I already knew what I wanted to do. I was running on a well-honed instinct. I was running on a will that had been shaped by an even stronger woman before me and on thirty years of some of the darkest scenes life could throw at a person. The doctors didn't know I was a determined and resilient woman who had already lost one child and would be damned if she was going to lose another. They didn't know the things I had survived. They didn't know I had already made up my mind. If this was cancer, we were going to move aggressively to treat the cancer by removing the lump and even the breast, if necessary, but I refused to do chemo and risk harming my baby.

Days later I began to prepare for surgery. I was scared, but I had been scared for so long carrying a child that it freed me to do what was necessary. I was used to being scared. And so I carried the courage of all the people who had built me up. I was two people physically, but spiritually I was many more. I carried Grandmomma Witherspoon with me. I stood on their shoulders. I couldn't let the world see I was afraid. I couldn't let them know the nights I lay awake staring at the ceiling and wondering if I would survive. Wondering if I would ever bear a child who would survive. I couldn't let them know I still cried in the bathroom over Jordan and shook with the fear that after everything we had done to pull through his loss, I was now gripped by a disease that could carry me away, too. I could only be brave. I could only go on instinct. I could only trust in God.

The day of my surgery I was calm. It was a warm fall in Phoenix and as I drew my clothes around me to leave for the hospital I felt something move inside me that stilled my feet. For the first time I felt the first tiny kick in my stomach. I couldn't move I was so happy. Supreme hope filled my heart and my chest swelled with love. I knew everything was somehow going to be okay.

Later at the hospital the nurses prepared me for surgery. Before they drew me back the doctors performed a final scan of the operating area, and as they scanned my chest there was a sudden stop.

"Well," I heard one of them say.

Few things make you worry like a nurse caught off-guard. I was starting to get tired of that feeling, and I pressed her for an answer.

"Well now I'm looking here," she said, "and I don't even see a lump."

There was no surgery. There was no lump.

* * *

Labor that spring proceeded as normal. Everything was fine and we were gripped by joy knowing we were so close to making it, knowing I was so close to having protected a child that was part of me.

Michael held my hand as I prepared to deliver and we were anxious with hope. My friend, Rita waited patiently with us in anticipation of our great bundle of joy. Every minute carried us to the other side of our grief. But not long into the delivery there was a pause. Suddenly a nurse brushed by Michael and strapped an oxygen mask around my head. I was intense with adrenaline. No one explained what was happening. Things turned urgent. Michael could only watch.

Immediately two doctors rushed in the room and flipped me over. The baby was not breathing. I was wheeled out of the room, quietly in fear.

"Ma'am," a doctor said. "Ma'am, we need to know: Do you consent to an emergency C-section?"

We were pushing toward another room, and I could hear my breathing in the mask. I was in the middle of the delivery. My child was so close within me. We were six inches from life. I couldn't endure God taking another life from inside me. I couldn't bear it. Not again.

In the days after Jordan's loss, back when I was beaten down with grief, there were times I wasn't able to understand how we would ever pull out of it. When Michael and I looked at each other we no longer saw only a pure, unadulterated love. We saw pain in each other's red eyes. We saw an emptiness we didn't know before. We roamed our own house locking away clean, plastic toys and newly pressed baby clothes in closets we would never open.

Michael was the only person I had to lean on in those days. He wanted so badly for us to be able to find healing, and so he pretended he was fine and went back to work, because he had to. I could picture him at his computer, looking out a window in quiet sadness or glancing at a picture of the two of us and knowing things could never be the same. I could see his co-workers innocently ask how I was doing. I saw him put on smiles to get through it. He had to take these bullets for our family. That was the burden he assumed.

Michael called me often in those early days to check on me. One morning not long after he had gone back to work we spoke on the phone and he quickly sensed something in my voice he didn't trust. Something was not right. Without understanding it, he felt drawn to help me and hung up the phone to rush home. He found me in a ball on the floor of our shower. I had already delivered Jordan—in pieces—by the time he got there. Michael carried me out and from the bedroom floor I watched him go back in and close the door behind him so I would not have to see.

I don't remember saying it, but a nurse told me later the only response I gave back to the doctors was, "I want my baby to live," over and over as we wheeled down the hallway.

There was no time to administer additional painkiller for the operation, and I endured it with only my epidural. The pain of giving life seared through me, excruciating and hallucinatory. I lay on my back in agony as the doctors pulled me apart. After a moment they took something out and rushed away. I couldn't see. I only lay there, vulnerable and exhausted and completely with hope for a healthy child.

It was over fast. I closed my eyes and took deep breaths. Another child was gone from inside me and the emptiness left behind took my sense of life away. I had harbored two lives within me, lost one, and felt another taken away. I didn't know if the baby was dead. I didn't know anything. I held Michael's hand as the doctors began to stitch me together. I wanted him to protect me as he had before, to shield me from it and endure the pain for me. I wanted him to take the burden from me. But I knew he could not.

There was no way to make anyone understand the way it felt, to have had a life tied to your very soul and then, in a heartbeat, ripped out and run off. There was no way to make them understand what losing Jordan felt like. There was no way to tell them I was a mother without a child to prove it. There was no way to comprehend losing another. There would be nothing left of me.

As I lay still Michael stroked my hand. Recovery would be long. The process of two pregnancies had exhausted so much of my emotions and taken such a toll on my body that it was impossible to tell what would come back and what was lost forever. I was in intense pain and just wanted to be quiet. After what seemed like minutes, but in reality only seconds, the door opened and a nurse entered. I could see something in her arms.

I would hold her for a long time that day, and for many days after. I would look at her and think of a baby abandoned in a hospital years earlier and feel a surge of protection over her. I would come to know what it meant to feel you would die so that someone else would live. I would find out soon after that she was two minutes from being born brain dead. I don't know how close we were to losing the rest of her. But she was more beautiful than anything I could imagine. She was ours.

We would have many more days to hold her. We would have many more days to reckon with the way she made us feel. We would have a lifetime to heal together. We would have a lifetime to find hope in her.

The nurse smiled as she extended her toward me.

"Mrs. Cornelius," she asked, "What is her name?"

"Olivia," I said.

Four

Abandoning Camelot

We received so many gifts in Olivia's birth. Her presence gave us hope. Her smile gave us healing. Her laugh gave us life. It was almost as if we were born anew alongside her. We would never be the same people we were before Jordan, but in this new life we bore at least we knew our family would continue. This little piece of us that we never thought we would recover had been found.

The first months we had her felt like the first months of our marriage again. Everything that happened to us, everything we did, was all laid against the backdrop of supreme joy. My longing for children, so unfulfilled and so painfully stolen away was satisfied in her. She was our first mark of legacy. She would be the new thing we lived our lives for. The gifts my grandmother had given me would be given to her. And even if she would be the only child we held, she would be enough.

But of course she would not be the only child we held. Our family journey was nowhere *near* finished. Weeks after Olivia's first birthday, Michael enrolled in a PhD program in San Antonio and we headed east. He had discovered this thing inside him that needed fulfilling, found a desire he needed to chase, and of course I was completely willing to journey with him.

Somewhere inside me I still held the desire to continue my career as a successful businesswoman, but after I had Olivia everything I could love was wrapped up in my family. I was far from the communications degree and the editing desk I had left in Nashville. A growing marketing career had begun and balancing family, being a stay-at-home mom, and a growing marketing consultancy was exciting and exhausting. I knew Jordan and Olivia had made me stronger, but I wasn't sure what that would mean for my career going forward. I had seen darkness—looked it in the face, even—and had come out the other side a survivor. Not everyone else had this strength, and I know it could be put to use. The joy Olivia gave me could, too.

Less than a year into our time in San Antonio, Michael resigned from the PhD program and our journey began again. We spent many months afterward searching for things we could not find. It was frustrating, knowing our greater purpose was out there somewhere and not being able to grasp it. I still felt my life was building to a crescendo where my passion would meet my purpose. And I had found that in my family. And we were discovering it in our careers.

Thankfully, we held so much joy in the family we were building. Because we wanted another son or daughter to be close in age to Olivia, we had already decided to have another child by the time we moved to Texas. And on New Year's Eve, just a few months after we arrived in San Antonio, I burst with joy at the news again. She would be due in August.

I acted out my first two pregnancies very differently. With Jordan I set out to prove I didn't have to be a pregnant woman people felt sorry for. With Olivia I only wanted to survive. With Kristian, I no longer had to be afraid. I walked every day with her. I could finally turn my face to the breeze and feel confident in my ability to protect her. I decided early in the pregnancy to complete a half-marathon with her, and five months in I flew to Nashville and did it. I was joyful and confident and secure.

As her older sister had been a symbol of survival, she would be a symbol of *life*. I wanted life to course through her, to echo out of every step we took together, and so I made an intentional decision not to put it on hold while I had her inside me. I was joyful to be having another girl and together we passed the pregnancy milestones uneventfully. I didn't much fight it when I was told she would need to be delivered by C-section—a well thought-out plan was something I liked to hear with a pregnancy—and by the time her delivery neared I knew we were going to be okay, because I had endured everything a pregnant mother possibly could.

When I stopped feeling her move, I began to fear I would have to endure it all again.

It was unusual for Kristian to hold still inside me. We had been so zealous and active and confident together. By that point I had honed a flawless ability to tell when something was not right with my body. On a Saturday morning right before her arrival, with Michael outside doing yard work, I was forced to fall once again into the heart-drop of something gone wrong. I couldn't feel her. I ran through the protocol of it, first drinking something cold, then eating something sugary, trying to get her moving again. I lay on my left side to increase her oxygen, praying, waiting, knowing any second she would once again pound to get out. But the stillness inside me stopped me cold. I couldn't breathe with fear. When Michael came in the house I was in quiet tears. Within minutes we packed a bag and left for the emergency room.

The ultrasound showed us that her kidneys had failed. Again, almost unbelievably, I found myself staring at a cold hospital wall as the words "emergency C-section" rattled around my brain. Again, just *steps* from the finish line, the precious time spent with my child inside me would end with a fast surgery. My running partner, my walking buddy, my symbol of life, was in need of rescue. So once again I would forego the romance and beauty of bringing a child to life in order to merely keep her alive. Once again I closed my eyes in prayer and was met with nothing but silence.

The days before, Michael and I had attended the Southern Baptist Convention in San Antonio. I still harbored many connections from my days at LifeWay in Nashville and the conference was a chance to reconnect with many people I knew. I had spent much of our year in Texas focusing on being Olivia's mom, so wherever our next stop would be I figured we would be there because of Michael. A full time career was in my backseat.

Because Michael was no longer in the PhD program, our health insurance was set to run out in two weeks. Kristian, of course, did not care about our health insurance or our income and was twenty-four hours from her arrival. We had enough time left on our insurance for the delivery, but not for all of her wellness visits after that. When we looked into the weeks and months ahead all we saw were medical bills and the giant unknown. We had thought our move to Texas was going to be the next stepping stone to our life's purpose together, but as we walked the floor at the Convention it was hard to know why we had even been *brought* to San Antonio. It was exciting rather than scary to look into our future even though we could only see a dark tunnel. I thought about these things as I walked through the conference with a belly about to burst. But those thoughts were confirmed minutes later when an old co-worker approached and without warning offered me an editing job back in Nashville.

Working again for another company was one of the absolute last things on my mind with a baby about to arrive. But his words flipped on something inside me. We had been so obsessed with finding what our next step was, so paralyzed with indecision, that the chance to just add some sort of motion to our plan was a turning point. But I knew editing wasn't my passion anymore and I wouldn't be happy doing it. So I turned down the offer. But we still needed motion. So before I left, with a sense of nothing to lose, I asked about any open marketing positions.

Of course, just hours later, my only thought was Kristian's survival. Unlike with Olivia, this time the doctors had monitored the two of us overnight and set a schedule for the delivery. Though it had its snags, there was still a plan. And the morning after I felt I had lost her inside me, she came back to us, loud and messy and beautiful. Her birth felt cold and bare. But her presence filled our lives with warmth.

She was the second six-pound, five ounce baby girl I had delivered. She was the second nineteen-inch baby girl I had delivered. The first words I heard about her would be the same ones I would hear in so many weeks to follow. Michael was the first to say them, always the first to hold our babies, and I knew when it came out it would mark her as ours.

"Wow," I heard him say. "She looks *just* like Olivia."

They were identical, down to their Apgar scores and the shades of their skin. And the feelings of joy and purpose they brought were, too. In a weird way, the similarities provided us great comfort. In a world of unknowns, it was something we could understand. These pregnancies had become little pictures of our lives. Every journey would take its own winding path to its own resolution. We could have no way of knowing how we would get to the end. But somehow we always did.

The Friday after Kristian's birth I was offered a marketing position back in Nashville. The chance to continue our journey east and move back closer to family was there if we wanted it. Looking back now I wonder if I should have thought about it more, or reckoned with how it would feel to return there. But I never did. So much had changed; my life—my family—was so different. After a lifetime of much loss, I had found a life that afforded me gain. I had left Nashville a single, wide-eyed, hopeful girl head over heels for a boy out west. I would return older, and affected. A different person in every possible aspect. I had seen how hard life could be when it veered off your tracks for it and how delicate hope can be given in a rush and taken back in an instant.

I never thought about the clapboard house, or walked down the sidewalks in my mind. I didn't see Arthur Avenue when I closed my eyes. We had sold six different homes since I left Nashville; it didn't even feel like my own past. God, I had spent so many years growing into the person I was meant to be. I had *clawed* out. Graduating college was so hard and meant so much. It was the first step in becoming something of myself—the first time I could put my childhood behind me and become a new woman. And I *had* become a new woman. I never once in the process considered that I was going home. Home was my husband and daughters, whether we were in Arizona, or Texas, or a van somewhere between. It wasn't Nashville. We were just moving to another city. And so we buckled in two car seats and the four of us headed east again, San Antonio to Nashville, still chasing the right key to open our doors and wondering every day if that key could really be in the first place I left it.

Those years were such a whirlwind that some days the only way to remember where we had been was to look at the two girls in the backseat. Our kids were the souvenirs of each place we lived. Olivia represented Arizona; Kristian was a parting gift from Texas. We were in no immediate hurry to collect another in Tennessee.

Being back there felt so different. Going to a place you have left can feel weird if the place has changed. But it wasn't so much that Nashville had changed, it had—and *I* had. The same buildings and streets I had left years earlier sprawled back before me, but I saw them differently. In my mind, I was completely divorced from the past I had left before. We bought a large home in a gated suburb thirty minutes outside the city. We shopped and ate in places I could have never imagined as a child. The only time I spent in the actual city was on its interstates and in a high-rise office that overlooked downtown.

When I first left Nashville for Arizona, I didn't view it as fleeing my past or escaping from someplace I didn't want to be. I had been happy there before. But there was something about that time away that changed me. I had become something, made good on the sacrifices invested in me, had accomplished so much, and wasn't a little girl anymore but a woman with two little girls of her own. I left the city as Dawn Witherspoon and returned as Dawn Cornelius—stronger, more secure, more accomplished, and moved on.

I found purpose in work, and soon Michael did, too, and for the first time we were able to ride to work in the same car, to offices separated only by a few steps down the hallway. We loved working together. Life was good. We had decided; now well into our thirties, that we would not have any more biological children, and until we were able to satisfy our calling to adopt our family of four would stay that way. After five years and three states, the time to create consistency and plant some roots had hit.

About two years into our time back in Nashville, with our lives on cruise control, an odd pattern started to emerge in the relationships I had formed. More and more it seemed the conversations I had were bending toward the same topic. It wasn't something I was seeking. In fact it wasn't something I felt I even needed to consider, but a funny little concept began to infiltrate the conversations I held with friends. Little by little, I began to realize the bounty of time I spent talking to those around me about the concept of legacy.

These new conversations pricked my heart with a different idea. Rather than balance my decisions against the immediate impact they would bring, I became obsessed with seeing them zoomed out, part of a bigger picture. The day-to-day began to wane, and the canvas began to come into focus. Our lives, I was beginning to realize, were bigger than just the twenty-four hours in front of us. It was amazing how frequently I began to talk about it. Our girls were getting older, our careers were taking new shape, and our lives were on a straight road. It was being made clear to me that the thing to do now was to look at what we would leave behind. As the conversations began to pile on top of one another, the pricks turned to full-on prods. Michael was the only male in his family. And I knew he wanted a son.

This idea of legacy wasn't new to me; since I recognized my grandmother's impact on my life I felt the importance of it. But it wasn't until I got older and our spare rooms turned to nurseries, and our nurseries turned to playrooms, that I saw a place in my life for it. Michael and I were no longer living for ourselves. We were starting to sow seeds that would be passed to the ones who would carry on our names. Olivia and Kristian were key to me seeing that. But it wasn't until we took a trip to Ecuador that it really became manifest in my life. I had been on mission trips before, but there was something about this one that was different.

God had pricked my heart with a specific word on the flight over on a previous business trip to Las Vegas about a man of faith named Ezra, whom the Bible said was "determined in his heart to study God's Word." I couldn't shake that description during our time there—it was such a picture of who Michael and I wanted to be. It was the exact image of who we wanted our kids to be. To determine in our heart to study God's Word. I couldn't get over it.

It wasn't the only thing I couldn't get over. While in Ecuador, I struggled to shake jet lag. Something just felt wrong. There's always a risk of catching a bug when you travel overseas, but this wasn't that. I felt flipped upside down on the inside, unable to shake whatever it was that had me. I was tired and felt bad. Finally, after a few days, the only thing I could tell Michael was either I was dying or I was pregnant. Either way I was going to have some news.

A quick pregnancy test after we arrived back home in Nashville confirmed it: That man of faith, the one we so longed to model? We were going to have a real good chance to get to know him. Ezra would be due in February.

You learn a lot about yourself in four pregnancies. You learn what your body can handle and what it can't. You learn what to do and what not to do, whom you should listen to and whom you should ignore. Most of all you learn about the child you're bringing into the world. Olivia was calm and measured, like her father, careful and meek. Kristian was a firecracker, busy and active, and she came out to kiss the world on its cheek, so ready to begin life that she made the doctors deliver her a few days early.

Ezra was a quiet baby. I took three or four trips to the doctor during my time with him just to make sure he was okay. He hardly moved inside me at all. I had always tried to interpret my kids' behavior in the womb, but I didn't know how to read him. Would he have health problems? Would he struggle with his development?

We were so joyful to be having a son. I knew what it meant to Michael—this boy would carry our name on to the world after we were gone. He would be the Cornelius that endured, as Michael had and his father had before him. To have our own little piece of family legacy was unbelievable. The chance to rear this boy would change all of our lives. But what kind of boy would he be? He was so still. I was four months on with him before I even *knew*. In the five months after, there were many days I wouldn't have known if the woman I saw in the mirror hadn't told me.

My doctor told me early in the pregnancy that this time I would have the option to deliver him by natural birth if I preferred, and I was thrilled. Olivia and Kristian had been born in such sterile, risky circumstances; the chance to bring our little boy into the world as God intended filled me with hope. That would mean something. It would be our triumph, the pretty little bow that would wrap up our family. I definitely wanted a natural birth.

As we neared term, Ezra continued his peaceful existence, but I found it increasingly difficult to carry him. It was hard to stand or move for extended periods of time. Things were painful. It felt like I was trying to support a bowling ball on a rubber band. I felt a heavy, sagging pain. I couldn't be up for more than five minutes, and I soon went on a long bed rest.

The closer February got the more I wondered if we needed to bring him in as the others had, just to be safe. The more I labored, the more I felt it had to be done. In the end, he was all that mattered, not how he got here, and so we set his C-section for February 2, 2010.

The delivery was as smooth as it could possibly be. For the first time my C-section didn't feel clinical; for the first time I felt no worry in my child's arrival. Everything had been planned with a procedural accuracy down to the minute. He came a noisy bundle of joy, small and compact with a push-button nose and his dad's eyes, with slick hair and a fair complexion. Once again his father was the first to declare his beauty.

It was freezing outside the day of Ezra's birth. But I had never known such warmth. Lying in the bed afterward, holding him close to me, I wondered what I missed in my life being unable to naturally birth any of my children. I couldn't imagine what that must have been like—to use your body in all its intention, as your mother had done before—I had never known it. Maybe it would have been worth it to try with Ezra. He would be my last chance. Maybe we had been too cautious. His presence gave me such assurance that he would have been alright. We were so filled with joy to have him. But I wondered what I had missed.

Later that afternoon the doctor came to check on me. "Well, everything went really well," he said, and then I noticed something in his face I hadn't seen before.

"But Dawn I have to tell you, it's a good thing you opted for a C-section."

Michael and I looked back at him puzzled. He spelled it out for us. The reason for my pain? The sagging difficulty we couldn't understand? There was something there they hadn't known, and the bed rest and the heaviness was all for good reason. My rubber band, he told me, couldn't hold that bowling ball.

"We didn't realize you were close to experiencing a uterine rupture," he said.

Michael and I looked on in shock and disbelief. I held Ezra close. One or both of us could have been lost if we tried a natural birth. The doctor talked through what it meant, but I didn't need a medical explanation. I looked at my son's eyes and finally understood. I finally heard what in his silence he had been telling me. I'm gonna lay real still, he had said, and we'll get through it just fine, mom. I'm gonna be your helper when I get there, and so for now I won't move much and we'll make it through this together.

"Somebody must be looking over you," the doctor said.

But he didn't have to say it. I already felt it. He had determined in his heart to study God's word, and determined in his stillness to save his mother's life.

* * *

Bringing Ezra home meant three kids under the age of five. That's a chaos you can't really explain. Trying to wrangle two little girls and a newborn is kind of like trying to grab on to a waterfall. Your whole world is just motion and screaming. My life was basically one long series of stains. Words like "silence" and "peace" became relative. Sleep was a myth, something I vaguely remembered once getting to experience. There were no more heartfelt conversations about whether we wanted to have another child. One typical day with our three told us everything we needed. Besides, had we even wanted to have a serious conversation in our house it would have ended with someone running through the room naked and someone else getting hit in the head. We were good for a while.

Our home in Nashville was in many ways a sign of my achievement for others who viewed us. For me, it was just a home. My grandmother's house could have fit in our family room. We were so grateful to be able to give our kids this *castle*—to let them run and scream and hit each other until they collapsed in exhaustion, and never have to leave the upstairs to do it. They wouldn't have to kick rocks down the sidewalks of our street.

Driving up to the stone edifice of our neighborhood was like driving up to Camelot. It was *stately*. Its appearance carried weight. These kids and this house were beginning to form our picture of legacy. Olivia and Kristian and Ezra would be it for us; they were the ones to carry all this on. And life in the house was fun for a while. But the more we thought about it, and looked at the things around us, the more uncomfortable we became with just what they would be carrying.

Sunday mornings had a lot to do with it. Getting ready for church in our house was like wrestling squirrels. Between the socks, the shoes, the dresses, the potty breaks, the other socks, the wrong shoes, the second potty breaks, the breakfast, the breakfast stains, the second dresses, the third potty breaks, and the car seats, the whole endeavor was like trying to dress cats for a wedding. By the time we were all in the car I had no idea if one of them was upside-down or stark naked or belonged to the neighbors. "Just go," was all we could say.

I can't imagine what we looked like rolling into church. Our car was like a self-contained Mardi Gras parade—you never knew what was going to come out when you opened the door. Would someone be dressed like a cowboy? Would a dog run out? Would someone be throwing handfuls of crayons and crackers out the window? We were a rolling carnival.

Many Sundays, inevitably, the nursery would be closed and that carnival would carry over to the pew. In many ways I never prayed more than when the kids sat with us—the word "sat" being used very loosely, there—usually beseeching Almighty God that my daughter would keep her clothes on until the final "amen" allowed us to bolt back outside. It was very spiritual. There were lots of chances to ask for forgiveness, such as when Kristian would stand on her head in front of God and everyone and flip her dress upside-down. I can't imagine the willpower it took for our pastor to not make eye contact with us. Going to church should not require two straight hours of apology when you pull in the parking lot, but I'm sure God got real used to it when He saw us coming.

Sunday mornings just defeated us. By the time we got home, and the shoes and dresses and socks came off for good, the energy we spent and the spiritual nourishment we were fed canceled out into a net gain of absolutely nothing. We'd come back to the house and just lie around exhausted. No one had been fed, no one had been clothed, and no lives had been saved. Had an alien landed and watched our family on Sunday morning, he would have thought church meant a four-hour family wrestling match that ended in a heap on the couch. We struggled with Sunday mornings. Some Sundays were an extension of everything we did from Monday to Friday.

We spent about three hours in the car on an average day, driving to daycare in the morning then thirty miles to work, then coming back in the afternoon and collecting the kids back up so we could hit the garage door opener as fast as possible. To run errands, grab groceries, and squeeze in doctor visits meant getting back in the car and getting back out. The kids were basically extensions of their car seats. There was no time to spend with them in the mornings—they had to get clean and brush their teeth and get dressed and hurry their bottoms to the car so we could get them to daycare. Everything we did was on a continuous treadmill we could not stop.

Something was changing in us. Our need for community began to bring to light all the places it didn't exist. Sunday mornings and get-togethers with friends started to become a symbol for a clear unsettling of our hearts. Our neighborhood was basically just a chain of islands—perfectly manicured lawns and isolated families who rarely ventured outside. Everyone had their own little world. When we took walks on Saturday mornings we were the only people out on the street. Our house had a beautiful deck that never got used. The sounds I was used to growing up, the rhythm of the city and the life that buzzed among it, were foreign to our kids. The predominant sound of their outdoor childhoods was silence. It was as if they had an empty world to themselves. This perfect place came at the total cost of community.

It wouldn't make sense to an outsider. It *really* wouldn't make sense to an outsider who knew my story. This place we lived wasn't just unimaginable to a kid on Arthur Avenue—it was off limits. Neighborhoods like this just weren't part of your reality. And to break free of that, then endure the pain and loss we had all while building toward successful management careers? We had more than earned the right to live there.

I hadn't thought that was a problem before. My family, my ministry, and my work were all I ever *wanted* to be happy with. But the stress of maintaining them was robbing away any joy they were bringing. I started searching Scripture for the feelings I was having. Michael and I spent long hours talking about it. What we felt was something you heard about, not something you looked out for. But we were definitely there: our lives had control of us. We were captive to everything we had built.

In a way it was a lot like being pregnant. We're all pregnant with something, whether it's an idea, a notion, a dream, or restlessness. It keeps you up at night. You can't enjoy food. You think it's external, but really it's internal, sitting inside you, impossible to ignore. And as it develops, it takes up more space than it used to, until it *consumes* you. I had been pregnant with things before—love, dreams, and children—but now I was pregnant with something very different. I was pregnant with a restlessness that was forcing me to give it life.

We knew the house had to go. It was a symbol for everything we didn't like. It was too big, too expensive, and too far. We didn't want it. But it took being in it to know it wasn't for us. Had we never had it I think part of me might have always worked toward it. As it had been delivering my three babies, I might have wondered what I had missed out on. But the point of those three C-sections was not that something had been stolen away from me; it was that I had found purpose in something different. And so it was with the house. Those Sunday afternoons and Monday mornings told us everything we needed to know. Our eyes had been on the wrong thing.

Houses are a symbol in my life—symbols of things I have left, and things I have earned. But this house was a symbol for something else. At first it meant achievement, but by the time we left it only meant misguidance. We spent a long time packing it up and even longer looking for where we'd go next. The sprawl of the city offered any choice of suburbs where we could have hidden, but we knew we wouldn't find what we were looking for there. The heart of the city was returning to its interior. If we were going to be true to this thing inside us, our search had to start there. And I knew what that meant.

There were only a few neighborhoods I was willing to go. Many places were off limits. There still needed to be a buffer to certain parts of the city, so if we had to be *in it*, we didn't have to be *all the way* in it. The neighborhoods we looked at were soaked in upscale modernity and polished gentility and had buzzy names like 12 South and Green Hills. We canvassed the perimeter for months, still not finding the thing we were missing. At a certain point Michael and I had to accept it: at its root, this move was about one thing—one *simple* thing—and if we weren't going to look for that, if we weren't going to be true to our search for community, then we might as well stay in Camelot. Because that was the only thing that mattered in this search.

It was the first time either of us had considered voluntarily living inside a city. At this point in our lives cities simply weren't places where people lived. They were hubs that held the suburbs together—just places where you worked or ate. Community meant getting in the car and driving to the mall. But the more we became unsettled with where we were, the more we had to admit these definitions were changing. We weren't finding community in our definition. When Michael and I talked about it, we finally were talking about the same thing. My dreams were his dreams. We were finally sharing the same wavelength.

At this point Nashville was experiencing a rebirth of its urban community. Month after month the city was growing from the inside out. Small businesses and rejuvenated neighborhoods started to build a vibrant core that attracted young families who were all making this same decision. But even if I couldn't possibly deny the city I had left was the city I needed. I also couldn't deny that it still held a very specific symbolism to me. No one moves out of the city to move back into it. Every person who climbs out of poverty sees it in the same way: the place you leave behind becomes a symbol for that life you left.

As you can afford more you tend to buy more. And so we had. It wasn't ego; it's just what we did. And at every stop the houses that had cost the most were in the suburbs. In a very real way, going back meant abandoning this climb, and I wasn't sure what that was going to mean. But, we wanted community instead of status. We wanted to become a part of something.

Wealth's greatest power is that it gives you choices. That's all it really does. The only difference in someone with means and someone without is that the person with means has options. And the only difference in the Dawn of Tennessee State University and the Dawn of Camelot was that I had the freedom to decide what I wanted. And I had decided I wanted to push a stroller with my neighbors. I had decided I wanted to use our deck together, and stay off the interstate. I wanted to know the people I lived among and find ways to impact their lives, and when my neighbors walked in my house I wanted them to spill drinks and track mud and not worry that they were somehow insulting the fabric of everything we had built. I wanted *diversity*. I had looked at our lives and was voting for community. Slowly we inched our search inside the perimeter of the city.

When we first began to consider East Nashville, I realized how closely our kids would be raised to the place I had been raised. For the first time Nashville was that place I had left before. It was a city I had once known. The streets, the houses, were all familiar. I had been able to push it all out of my mind in the suburbs, but I couldn't look for a home among my old zip code and ignore what it meant. We were looking for a house ten minutes from Arthur Avenue.

I had kept two of grandmother's things from the old house. The first was a simple twelve-by-twelve throw pillow a cousin had made for her, embroidered with a picture of a grandmother on it. The second was a plastic grandfather clock she had bought for a few dollars. It was one of the few things she ever bought for herself, and I was with her the day she bought it. I will always carry that look on her face with me. I'll never see such pride again.

When she died, that house died. I didn't take my old report cards or school pictures. I didn't want the furniture or the plates or care what happened to the bedrooms and walls. I left her Bible on the dresser. Her death gave me permission to bury that place along with her, and everywhere I had lived since had been one rung up from where I had begun—one more stake in the ground to keep Olivia and Kristian and Ezra from having to know what it's like to live in a place like that. But here we were about to bring them closer to it.

We found a house a few miles away, and on a muggy summer morning we left the gate behind for good and made our home on Russell Street. Maybe they would kick a few rocks, after all. Maybe we all would. Maybe we would find the thing we were chasing. Maybe we would learn not just our neighbors' names, but how they took their coffee and what they called their grandparents.

I have learned now not to fear a search for something in life. We're always searching for something—it's just the thing we're searching for that changes. When I first left Nashville I was looking for happiness. Since then I had looked for hope, then comfort, then success, then security. I'm sure there will be a measured amount of searching until I die. We all do.

Moving downtown wasn't going to fix that. In many ways the search had just begun. Because when I reconciled this element of my past, and Michael and I traded our kids' posh suburban childhoods for community-soaked sidewalks, it changed the way I viewed our city, and after that came a change in the way I viewed the people *in* the city. Because Arthur Avenue was still there, and its houses were all still full.

Five

Good Begets Good

There are only a few ways you can handle your past. You can run from it, denying the things that happened to you and focusing only on the moment. You can spite it, and fill the pain with money, success, and achievement, using the anger that comes from having had to experience it to fuel yourself against it. You can feel sorry for yourself, pouring pity in your wounds and offering it to the world as something they owe you. Or you can tuck it away. You can know it doesn't define you and still keep a spot for it in your back pocket, because if you don't have to look at it every day you can still know one day you just might need it.

Our personal histories are no deader than we are. I had spent years throwing dirt on a living, breathing thing, and you can't bury something that's not been killed. I couldn't keep my past down until I faced it dead on and told it I no longer had to live by its definition of who I was. It took a deep desire for community to push me to do that. I had to want that more than I wanted to not be hurt by my past.

But in my search for community I discovered what I had endured as a child couldn't even hurt me anymore—I held things on my heart that built an armor against the pain. The numbers I was given by my family shielded me from it. They gave me hope, and joy, and love, and when I realized that, and we moved into a home minutes from the one I worked so hard to escape, our lives bloomed under the shadow of healing. I would always hold a testimony of poverty's grip, but I could finally, totally, honestly bury the fear I associated with it.

In many ways I thought that meant I had won. The things I had achieved—a family, a career, a community with a purpose—finally outnumbered the things I longed for. The scales had tipped in our lives. With each new relationship we formed in our city, with each week spent imbedding ourselves into the fabric of our neighborhood, our joy grew. And the further I got from it the more I realized my grandmother wouldn't have been proud of me for buying a big fancy house in a gated neighborhood thirty minutes from my problems. But I felt now she might.

At the same time, my career had evolved into form. While on maternity leave with Ezra I received a call from the Director of Publishing at my company asking if I would be interested in a managing director position over church publishing materials for student ministry. In time, I prayerfully expressed interest and wanted the position. It would halt much of my travel from the marketing world and afford me the chance to lead—to build business concepts and think big picture while leading a healthy team. I took baby Ezra to a friend and spent the first day of our lives apart interviewing for the position. On May 1, 2010, I became the second woman to be a managing director at the company.

The job brought great fulfillment. I had long harbored a dream to build things that stretched back to my *Greatbusiness.net* days. I had felt then the rush of creation—the energy that came from starting something that worked—and in the day-to-day management of our department I held the chance to do it all again with a much larger support network around me. I organized dream retreats for our team, I encouraged outside-the-box concepts, and I reinforced the power of *now*. With the thrust of a large corporation behind me it sometimes felt the entire world was laid out before us. The possibilities to create change had never looked so vibrant.

Part of my job involved giving dynamic presentations of our products to different groups. I did this a lot and had it down to something of a art—the right balance of story, strategy, innovation and relation always got the job done.

In fall 2011, after I had been on the job almost eighteen months, I was asked to speak at an urban think-tank at work. It was mostly a chance to expose our publishing materials to a new market. As the managing director our publishing unit, I had done dozens of these spills and was eager to do it.

Because the audience was a group of urban leaders, I decided a little of my story could create a bridge of understanding and relation from them—maybe how I had found hope in the leaders of my church as a child, deftly segued into how valuable *our* resources could be in the hands of people who can make a difference. *I grew up in this city's urban environment, and found a safe haven in our community church*, I'd tell them. *Your kids can, too. Now...here's our resources connect?*

I ran through my story and finished the presentation. I didn't think much of it and was happy for the chance to meet them and if we gained new customers out of it all the better. As I was packing to leave a man got up from the group and approached me. I noticed he had an urgency about him. He introduced himself as Anthony. He was a polished thirty-something, clearly successful at whatever it was he was doing. I happily shook his hand.

"I just wanted to meet you," he said. "I'm from the Urban Youth Workers Institute."

"Hi Anthony, it's nice to meet you," I offered back. I figured he was about to ask about a specific product or ministry strategy and I readied for an explanation.

"I just wanted to tell you what your story meant to me."

My story?

"The things you said about your grandmother, and your childhood. I was blown away by that. That's incredible."

I paused, caught off guard.

"I was wondering if you would be willing to share it with our organization," he said, "at our next board meeting in California." I was humbled and intrigued. "We will gladly take care of everything, fly you out, take care of hotel accommodations, and it would really mean a lot if you would."

My story wasn't something I normally shared—certainly not a normal part of business presentations—and not because I was afraid of it, but because I didn't see any real point in sharing it. In no way did reckoning with my story give me the power to start using it to affect other people. It only gave me the power to use it to affect myself. When it came to other people, I didn't think it was any better than the stories each of the 7 billion of us already held. The only reason I had shared it that morning was the captive audience I thought it might resonate with. I didn't see any power or call to action in my testimony. I didn't even see it as a *testimony*. It was just me. And I had lived in my skin so long that it certainly didn't seem anything special.

I told Anthony I would be happy to consider it if my schedule would allow. But the call came in November: I would fly to California for two days. The UYWI Board of Directors would meet in a large house on the beach outside Los Angeles. The only thing I was to do was to stand in front of them and tell the same story I had told at the think-tank.

I took my seat on the plane with a feeling I had never known before. I traveled often but generally to speak, lead conferences, lead a marketing effort, meet authors, navigate a business deal, or to evaluate a new business opportunity but never because someone has invited me to talk about my personal story.

I met Anthony for lunch. After lunch we arrived at the house, tucked into a neighborhood that sat right on the Pacific Ocean. It was a bright and cool day in Los Angeles and the mist rolled off the water in a thin sheen that covered the deck. As the meeting began, Anthony introduced me to the board. They stared at me, smiling. And then he turned it over to me.

I told them of a hospital and a woman and a choice. I started with a commitment and a house and a set of twins who learned to shuck corn and stand up to drunks. I told of a promise and a failure and a victory and a legacy. I talked of dresses and quilts and clarinets. I told the only story I knew.

* * *

When I finished, Anthony told me I could wait on the beach behind the house and after the meeting we would go to dinner.

It was mild and quiet on the beach. I walked to the water and called Michael, then placed my feet in the sand and thought about where I was. Until this point, every professional opportunity I had experienced had come because of my knowledge or resumé or performance in an interview. I had earned each of my experiences. And here I had been brought to California and hosted at a board meeting for an entirely different reason.

I had some time to myself on that beach. As I reflected on what I was doing, it became unavoidable to think that to that Board of Directors in the house, my sole value was something I had not earned. My story was the only reason they wanted me. They didn't need my marketing expertise or my twelve steps for a healthier organization. They didn't care about my heart for entrepreneurship or the degrees on my wall. They had flown me across the country because I had a powerful story to tell. That was it.

I wasn't there out of my own doing. The people who invested in me, these heroes who spoke into my life and wrote this story, had brought me there. My power, my currency was the hope that story offered.

Alone on the beach, my attitude toward myself began to shift. I began to reason that if UYWI saw this much worth in my story then it was only a matter of time before others would as well. I began to see that it was my real resumé—my living resumé—and the best way to truly understand the woman I had become. I began to realize that if I were going to do this I would have to feel confident. I would have to feel worthy of the testimony I was holding. And standing on that beach alone, I felt a new confidence. I felt sure.

All of us have stories. I still didn't see completely how mine would stand out. I was beginning to see how it could bring value to people. I listened for a word, for some sort of encouragement, and only heard the waves, lapping at my feet in a peaceful rhythm that hushed the world around me. That restlessness we first felt a year earlier hadn't been killed. It was as alive as ever in me.

The problem had not been our church or our pastor or our faith. And it wasn't even just our house. Our hearts had very clearly been stirred toward something bigger than the lives we were living. We moved downtown thinking we had conquered it, but standing on that beach I knew: those tugs of uneasiness were just contractions. We were still very pregnant with something demanding to be born.

It all felt so undeniable and yet so unsure. I would go back home changed sure of this calling and ready to act. But would there really be anyone listening? Would anyone honestly care what I had to say? What would it mean practically to share my story—would that be a business, a job, a new career? I didn't know what it meant.

Most of all I didn't *feel* like I had been chosen. I felt small and ordinary. The beach was much bigger. I watched the waves break on the shore and reach toward me, crash and erase, crash and erase, in an up-and-back cadence that marked the time.

And then I heard my name called out. I turned back to the house and saw Anthony waving me back in with a smile.

The calendar flipped to 2012 with an energy I had never felt. New years have always meant new beginnings, but my trip to California just two months before had changed what a new year was going to mean. I had begun to share my story with those around me in little moments here and there and felt very tangible reactions to it. The embers of something real were beginning to grow.

I soon became restless at work. I was reading books by thinkers like Simon Sinek and doers like Blake Mycoskie that were stirring up things inside me. I began to learn about this thing called social entrepreneurship and threw out different *what ifs* with friends of mine. And I no longer felt the energy I had before when I walked in my office every morning.

It was hard to know that switch had been flipped—to feel, without much warning, the passion for a career sapped out by something new—and I soon called Anthony from Nashville so we could talk it through further. I needed him to walk me through the life planning process he had gone through earlier.

For four hours, in my office with the door shut, I had Anthony lead me through an accelerated version of his life plan. He helped me understand the difference in a career and a purpose and what my "major gates" to happiness were that led to the place where my passion would meet my calling. We worked through what my story meant and how it could speak into others' lives. The more we talked about it the clearer it became that the simple story I had shared with him months before—that day-by-day testimony I just called my life—would be the central focus of the rest of my work. By the end of our conversation it was clear to both of us: the first major gate I needed to be happy was social entrepreneurship.

I knew I could no longer work in publishing. All my years of marketing and publishing experience were going to be foundational in whatever I would plan next, but they could no longer be my endgame. The idea behind identifying your major gates to happiness is so that you can know when you discover them you're living in your true purpose. Of the five Anthony helped me identify—social entrepreneurship, global impact, influencing major influencers, financial security, and my kids' stability—my current job only checked two. If I was to be honest with myself and to this story I held, I would have to leave.

It wasn't going to be easy. The landscape of our office was changing and I knew there was a good chance some personnel moves were going to leave me with an offer for a lateral move or major promotion.

I knew turning that down would be hard. I thought maybe there would be some benefit to accepting it, to grow my own platform and add to my income as I reckoned with this new calling and figured out what I was going to do, but Anthony saw it through a much more black-and-white lens.

"Dawn," he said before we got off the phone, "you're going to have a tough decision to make. You may be offered a significant job, but if it's outside these gates, outside your ultimate fulfillment, you're going to have to say no."

Easy for you to say, I thought. He *knew* what he wanted to do—and he had a whole team of investors behind him. So my major gate was social entrepreneurship. That didn't mean I had any *clue* what that was going to look like. I had three kids at home less than six years old, and a new house, and a potential new position knocking at the door. My entire life had groomed me to find these opportunities and say yes. I was a director at a major publishing company. This new direction not only ran counter to my situation; it ran counter to everything I had grown to believe.

A few weeks later I got a call and was told I would be offered another leadership position at our company. I searched the timing to find some idea of what it meant. Maybe the offer was a sign that the company was still where I was supposed to be. Maybe it was God telling me I would find fulfillment in where He had me. To be honest, I didn't know. I looked for signs in every angle of it and could have justified the decision either way. But the offer was on the table. And still unsure of what my newly discovered life plan would mean, I tentatively agreed to take it.

I had mixed feelings about taking the opportunity. I didn't harbor any illusions that it would make me feel more fulfilled or happier in my work. I still held something in me I couldn't ignore. But I was learning about this dynamic that so many of us deal with, this pull of feeling called to do something but not being sure practically what it looked like. And I didn't know where I fit in that tug-of-war.

It's easy to say that when you discover your calling, every decision you have to make going forward should be true to it. You shouldn't do anything with your career that doesn't somehow move you closer to living that purpose. And Anthony had showed me that. But it's another thing entirely to have a concrete opportunity on the table. It's hard not to push that button. There were still just as many signs around me that I needed to leave, still just as much restlessness, but careers can be so delicate and so hard-earned. Promotions and rewards are so comforting. It's never easy to say no. And so I didn't.

Not long after the call, I was in a meeting with a friend, Jerry Shirer, in which I was sharing a marketing idea that would cost thousands but advance his wife, the author's new book project. His response was a simple, quick, obvious comment that would serve as a great catalyst for me.

"Let me tell you something an old man told me once," he said. "Of all the investments you can make in your life—in your career, in anything—the best investment you can ever make is in yourself."

Three months after I spoke to UYWI in Los Angeles, I told my company once and for all I would be leaving. On my last day I stood in my high-rise office on the fourth floor and looked out the wall of windows that faced north. From downtown my office looked toward Arthur Avenue. There were the sidewalks I traced with Shawn when we were younger. There was Jefferson Street and Rosa Parks Boulevard. There was the spray-painted water tower, and just west of it the new projects painted in the bright reds and yellows and blues of urban gentrification with garbage cans and shrubs and driveways that would have made us feel like kings and queens. I had spent a long time earning those windows and everything inside them. But I still couldn't see the house from there.

* * *

It's amazing what leaving your job will do for your sense of urgency. It was one thing to venture out on my own with a story I thought could impact others; it was another thing entirely to face three hungry mouths at 5 o'clock every night. The day I walked out of my office for the last time we lost the luxury of drawn-out dreaming and experimentation. We had to get going with whatever this thing was going to be.

The challenge was to use this little platform—my story—to somehow birth hope in others through social entrepreneurship. But we didn't know what that would look like. It might be a coffee shop or an art gallery or a bookstore or a soup kitchen. We didn't have a mission statement or a website or a plan. We didn't know what Nashville needed or the best way to serve the most people, or what my grandmother would have told us to do. But for the first time in years I could finally look at my reflection and know I was being true to everything I saw looking back at me.

When I looked at the whole picture and how my story could somehow fit into it, I began to see one very central idea at its core: someone birthed hope in me. That was the root of it all. Everything would have to grow out from there. And quickly it did.

It came fast, as ideas often do, in the shower. When I got out I took it right to Michael.

In 1907, a woman was born who changed my life. This woman would make a courageous choice to save two lives when she bore no real responsibility to do so. She made a decision, this woman, that would spark an impact that lived far beyond her own life. She committed to seeing this decision through and the hope born in her simple, selfless, God-inspired choice that day in a Nashville hospital would change more than just two little babies: It would change the world. And so my story did not begin in 1972. It began in 1907.

We would call it 1907 Apparel. But it would not merely be a retail store; it would be a place that birthed hope as Olivia Witherspoon did, by carrying brands and causes that created their own hope in others. We would be the hub where these networks came together, the host that gave them a platform and a voice. We would find these people who were changing the world; we would invest in their message; and we would offer a place where they could all fit together under the same roof. We would give a portion of the money these causes brought in to local organizations that were changing our own community. Good would beget good.

We would center on one idea: anybody—any race, any income, any background—can take nothing and make something out of it. And we would focus on three ways. All would come from her.

The first would be poverty. Olivia Witherspoon knew poverty like no one else I knew in my life. She was born in it, raised in it, limited by it, and yet *never* beholden to it. It took unimaginable courage for her to do the things she did to survive. But she had already overcome poverty, because she had looked it in the face and declared she was better. There were more like her out there. We would do everything we could to help them break those bonds.

The second would be education. There is no greater weapon in the fight to succeed. No amount of money, no genes, no predetermined course for your life is more valuable than an education. My grandmother would have died for us to go to school, because that was what it was worth to her. Education saved my life. It gave me power like nothing else could. And it is a *birthright.* Every person deserves an opportunity to have a great education. We would take that very seriously.

The third would be sustainable agriculture. My grandmother's garden was the first model of social entrepreneurship I ever knew. She grew to give away. Not out of her bounty or excess, but out of principle. Alongside education, eating healthy is the most pressing crisis of underserved neighborhoods. Obesity and diabetes are at epidemic levels in many communities. This would be a major priority.

By focusing on these three causes, we could build a comprehensive plan to change our community. More importantly, we could ensure Olivia Witherspoon's legacy was honest to her life. They were the three tenants she raised us on; they were the three she devoted her life to. And she would have died before she compromised any of them. We would have to take that seriously.

One idea, three branches. It was simple, but transformative. Not unlike a woman I once knew.

The only thing scarier than quitting your job to follow your passion without a safety net is when the day comes you have to put your feet on the ground and start actually building that passion. When Michael and I looked at each other over the dinner table, we were looking at the only team we had. We no longer had an HR department, administrative assistants, managers and directors to lean on, or co-workers to help shoulder the load. We were the CEO, the CFO, the customer service department, the designers, the accountants, the web engineers, and the only thing it guaranteed us was that the Employee of the Month award would stay in our house each month. We quickly discovered we were going to need some help.

Though my story would be at the center of the 1907 Company, it would by no means be the only voice in the company. I had started small businesses before, both with small teams and by myself, but this was going to be different. The 1907 Company would become the founding social enterprise using commerce as a catalyst for change. Founded in March 2012, the 1907 Company would then launch two retail social enterprises bringing hope and change to thousands through the sale of cause-based brands and the companies' giving initiatives.

1907 Apparel was going to commit to being a platform for serious organizations around the world that were creating change. We had to have authority. Like my grandmother, we no longer just represented ourselves; every decision we made would ripple through the callings and passions of everyone who joined with us. The pressure was on us to get it right. And though I had total confidence in our ability to deliver, there was still a great responsibility in that. So Michael and I recruited a small team to help us.

We needed authoritative voices for the work we were doing; we needed people who would own it as we were. We needed people who were uneasy in their own work because they knew something bigger was out there and had the confidence to believe they had something worth contributing to it. In short, we needed *dreamers*. We found two, Adam and Scott, both young editors at the company I had just left, both of whom I had hired. After two lunch conversations, we doubled our workforce.

I left publishing for good in February. On March 1, 2012, the 1907 Company and thus, 1907 Apparel was born...

Launching a new business is a race against a dozen different things. You can't just let things happen as they will; you're up against your competitors, your market, and your savings account. We wanted the store to be open in six months, so the spring and summer would be a crash course in small business entrepreneurship. For everything we thought we needed, three or four things we had never heard of popped up. Codes and regulations and licenses loomed. And then there was the matter of finding a place to put the store. Where in Nashville would we be? Broadway? 12 South? The Gulch? East Nashville? Where could we afford? Where would make the greatest impact?

Adam and Scott began to build business relationships and develop marketing copy while Michael and I handled the larger nuts and bolts of opening a brick-and-mortar business. We dreamed long into the night. It was everything I wanted. I felt my major gates starting to open—*we* controlled what happened, not corporate bureaucracy. If we did something good, *we* got credit for it, not someone above us. If something needed to be changed on the fly, *we* did it with one call or email. We were lean and on fire. It was an energy I hadn't felt since my *GreatBusiness.net* days—a pulse you just don't understand until you're trying to hang on to it as it operates on its own momentum.

One of the first business decisions we made was to seek investments through crowdfunding—an exciting way to introduce an idea to the community-at-large by offering supporters a chance to fund a project they believe in. I had seen amazing projects funded through websites like Kickstarter and Indiegogo, and so I believed 1907 would fit in right alongside them. As Anthony and Adam and Scott and others had bought in, so too would everyone else. All they had to do was hear it.

Securing the capital we needed to finish the launch was critical, so we hired a videographer and filmed an in-depth interview with Michael and me about our story, as well as a promo video to market the concept. We needed this first impression to make an impact. After developing incentives and spreading the word to every breathing human being we all knew, we introduced the world to 1907 online with an ambitious goal of raising $40,000 to launch the business. One click and we waited.

Our crowdfunding campaign was a chance to find people who were willing to buy in to our idea, but in a larger sense it was our first impression on the community. I was optimistic about the funding, but even if we didn't hit $40,000 I knew we were pushing buttons that would resonate. My friends and family had reassured me: my story was transformative. Our crowd would see that. So we waited. I hit refresh, then waited some more, and hit refresh again. After a slow start I kept an eye on our total amount, watching for it to spring up with fresh support. But day after day it held close to the bottom. Two weeks into the campaign, we had raised only a few hundred dollars.

Somewhere there was a disconnect. Something in our message was not getting across. We tightened our language and made simple graphics and upped our incentives and kept hitting refresh. And the little green bar barely creeped at all. We went back again: our margins shrank, our expenses were reconfigured, our biggest dreams for the store went on hold, emails and tweets were sent, and we hit refresh again. But we could not poke that little green bar forward.

Our campaign lasted forty days. I had dreamed we would raise $1,000 a day to hit our goal, but after almost six weeks of crowdfunding we garnered forty-two founders for a total of $4,675. We had raised eleven percent of our goal.

Beyond the disappointment of not knowing where the money to open the store would come from, there was a sense after the campaign that something in our message was off. I began to ask hard questions about whether my story was worth the weight I had given it. Michael and I talked about the idea, running it over in our heads to see if we were handling it right, asking if the buy-in we expected was going to be there.

I thought for a while I had miscalculated. But as we kept on the road to opening the store, I learned something about our message: We hadn't brought a message to market people wouldn't believe in. The story *was* life-changing. We had just assumed people would buy in to it as easily as we had. But how do you describe to someone a retail store that's built on a story? You could argue—and we would agree—that in the traditional sense our store wasn't even really a *store*. How do you make that make sense in three sentences or less?

This was a dramatic lesson to learn early on, because it completely changed the way we approached our pitch. Before, we had assumed that because we knew my story inside and out, everyone else would be attracted to it as easily as we were. We thought a couple of videos and some promo pictures would be enough. But you can't assume your story is going to resonate. In many ways you have to treat your story like you're spelling it out to your own children, because that's the level of explanation and demonstration it takes to make it resonate in a loud market, where people are bombarded by thousands of pitches every day. It isn't pandering. The customer needs that explanation, or else the idea is washed away by the noise of the rest of the world.

We hadn't miscalculated my story at all. We just needed to sell it harder. After all, we were introducing a new idea to the consumer: a T-shirt that could be customized with your own number of hope on it— your own 1907, in other words—and worn out the door. It wasn't a natural transaction for people. It wasn't a familiar idea. It was completely new to our market and to our city.

Once we regained the faith in our story, the energy we felt in those early nights returned. We were bolstered by this sense that the story had to be sold harder than ever, because we knew that's what it would take. So that's what we did. And the million pieces scattered around us that would have to fall into place in order to get the doors open began, one by one, to do just that.

Soon we ordered our first shirt designs, developed our first partnerships and received our first product. We finalized logos, signed off on marketing copy, designed promotional materials, and were free from the burden of having to hit refresh. We were so thankful for the $4,675 we had been given and held it close to our hearts, stretching it as far as we possibly could. We would have to cash in our life-savings to do the rest. By the end of the summer we signed a lease for a storefront in a new development on a quiet street less than a mile from our house in East Nashville. Before long all that was left to do was paint the walls and open the doors—and then, after six months, finally do some work.

There was nothing in our old jobs that could compare to it. We were completely all-in on 1907 Apparel. There was no safety net. And yet I couldn't shake the feeling that, at the heart of it, this idea I was developing—this thing Michael and I and our own kids had all committed to—if it didn't work out, it wasn't the end of things. We could find other jobs. There would be other roads ahead. We felt like our idea could change the world, but at the end of the day we were still opening a business. It wasn't life and death. It wasn't our health.

And that line of thinking made the idea so much more real to me. Because my grandmother's commitment? It *was* life or death. She wasn't opening a store down the road from her house. She was saving lives. The stakes resting on our store made her stakes so much higher to me. She had made a snap decision that would change the rest of her life. How could one woman be that strong? How could she not think of the ramifications, or plan it all out on a spreadsheet? How could she not talk to her friends or her pastor about it? How could she just *act?* We lived and breathed our idea for six months just to open the doors. She saw something she knew was wrong and acted on it immediately. What a legacy to hold.

Thousands of small businesses open around the country every year, and to each of the business owners their little 40-by-40 box is a stake in the ground. They might be offering something to change the community, or something to change their families. They might be honoring a tradition, or offering a new one. For us, 1907 Apparel was a legacy move. Every position in business I had taken was answering the question; do I feel like I'm going to be part of changing the world? And in every position I was able to tell myself yes. It was a big deal to go back to work after being a mom—to drop my kids and head to an office, or to leave them behind to travel days at a time, but I was only able to do it because when I got home I could look at them and say: Mommy really thinks this is what God wants me to do to change the world.

When I no longer felt that way, I couldn't just abandon that principle for job security. I couldn't choose something I didn't believe was life-changing over my kids. That's why I left my job. And that's why, on October 23, 2012, when the doors to 1907 Apparel opened for the first time, on a crisp fall morning that cooled the store, I felt home again. Because I knew that night, when Olivia and Kristian and Ezra went to bed, I would be able to look at them and say: You might have to sacrifice some things for something you don't understand. You might have to go without. You might have to be the outcast, or the kid that feels different, and I know that is a burden you are not asking for. I know the way those glares feel.

But Mommy and Daddy really think this is what God wants us to do to change the world. This is what we believe He wants our family—all of us, even you—to commit to, because it is the gift and the burden we have been given. And we have to be true to that. And our family believes that if that means going without, or making a sacrifice, then that will be okay. Because we all have one life, one chance, to spread good news and hope to the world around us. And no matter what we have to go through, we will be a family that takes advantage of that one chance.

* * *

The early days of the store were taxing. The money coming in didn't justify the hours it took to keep the store running. But we were learning to expect that. So our margins got a little tighter, our message got a little firmer, and our relationships got a little more intentional. We knew down to the penny what it would take to keep our doors open, and we knew opening an apparel store less than three months before a Tennessee winter was probably not one of Dale Carnegie's principles of business. But our community—the small shops around us, the neighbors who became friends and the friends who became regulars—kept us so warm. We kept each other's lights on with the energy that we were all in it together. Whether we sold apparel or flowers or tea or candles, every one of us was in the same boat. That became such a gift as we felt our way through our first year.

Our model changed rapidly as we reacted to demand. As it is with any new business, some things worked and some things didn't. Some major dreams we had for the store had to be put off. Our priorities changed. As our sample size grew so too did the picture we received of what our customer actually wanted. And every night when I went home, thank God, I shared a bed with a market research guy who could help me understand it all.

Michael was critical at helping me navigate what we needed to do. Our energy in running the store was multiplied tenfold by the fact that we were getting to do it together. Every time we looked at each other across the store we saw ten years of memories in each other's eyes. We saw Phoenix and San Antonio and everywhere between. We saw sprinklers in a sunset park, and a whirlwind romance that would never have to end. We knew the secrets we held, the little things no one else ever would, and the promises we had made to each other. And every time we did, all it took was a soft smile to remind each other that there is no pain in life so costly as to not be healed by love.

One of the last pieces of the store that came together was a section of small framed photos that hung above the door. The door to 1907 is its threshold—the anchor frame of the wall and the strongest part of the building. It opens up to our street and carries great significance. Before the store opened we bought an old half-circle glass window to hang above it and I knew I wanted it filled with pictures.

I had the store to myself when I gathered the pictures to fill the window. I was exhausted with the store's construction. Everything had been a race. So much had to be done to get the store open that I hadn't had a chance to reflect on any of it. This one last piece was a chance to gain a final understanding of this thing we were doing.

One by one I slid them in—photos of the kids, photos of Michael and me, photos of family members who were important to our pasts. Each of them was a simple tribute to all the people we were doing this for. They smiled back at me as I settled them into place. God, I couldn't hardly recognize the girls. So much had changed. Michael's smile could always light a room with his beautiful and infectious smile. It was hard to imagine so much time had passed. Little by little they filled the window, in simple frames of thin gold, until there was only room for one more.

I held it in my hands for a moment. She looked ageless. It must have been a proud day for her, to sit in front of the camera in her best dress. She must have felt like a queen. Maybe groceries had been a dollar cheaper that month. Maybe she had just gotten her check. So unlike her, to have a photo like that. I still knew that smile. It felt as fresh as the day I first sounded out the third chapter of John.

I didn't have a fully formed picture of her that day back at the plantation. I couldn't know her sacrifice just yet. So sad that I hadn't wanted to go. So frustrating that I couldn't *want* that then. If Aunt Ada hadn't made me...if my father hadn't insisted...just hard to believe I was so unaware. If only I somehow could have bottled up the power I got retracing her steps in the dirt that day. I didn't need it then. When I did, I couldn't even remember it. To have had just a *taste* of it that night in the emergency room...to have been able to recall her there. I had needed her every day of my life.

That garden of hers, those pillbox hats. Her favorite pew at Mt. Bethel. I could never understand how many nights she fell asleep hungry. How unfair, for a woman so humble to be given such a lot. What a picture of hope. What a picture of love.

I never thanked her for those quilts. I never offered her my cornbread. She wore her knees raw praying for me. She bent down to the floor on worn-down joints that popped and ached, bone on bone, to kneel before God on my behalf. And this was the only place on earth that honored her.

I couldn't do the thing she did. I couldn't take those babies home. I couldn't devote my last twenty years to a split-second decision like that. But her story had always been my story. Her life had always been my life. She is what I always wanted to be. She is what we all can be. She is more than a grandmother; she is an idea, that we all have a story to tell. She is the symbol that everyone has the power to change someone's entire world, no matter how small or quiet or poor or old, because she hands-down *did it*. She is the thing that never gives up. She is the thing that endures.

I have messed a lot of things up. I have spent many years not feeling worthy of the things she believed about me. I have spent a lot of time running. But my heart has a home. And here, in a white half-circle frame in Nashville, Tennessee, is the thing that makes this place different. Because no one has what I have. No one has a picture of Olivia Witherspoon above the door.

After a moment I reached out my arms. I was crying as I slid the picture into place.

* * *

There are mornings I'll stand in the store alone, before it opens. Surrounded by merchandise—thousands of material dollars' worth of material things—I'll reflect on how, after the fights and failures and little victories of my life, everything I went through led me, almost precipitously, to a store.

A manmade 40-by-40 box next to a Vietnamese restaurant and a nail salon.

When I think of it that way, it seems my life has been leading me through seasons of pain and grief and fear just to put me in a box. A box of stuff. A box that sells merchandise Dawn Witherspoon never could have afforded. I try to make sense of it. I try to reconcile my search for purpose and worth with this place that search led me. I try to make sense of how it all led me to retail.

But in these quiet moments, in the mornings I look out onto Fatherland Street, I hear another voice. This voice doesn't care about my search, or this answer I have found, or where retail fits into things. This voice simply tells me to be quiet. To stop searching.

It tells me that the search was never about what I was looking for—it wasn't about the business or a salary or a magic bullet that waited for me at the end of the road—but that the search itself was the reward, and this thing I sought was there all along, and whether it ended with a store or a fancy office or three beautiful miracles who whisper in my ear before bed, I found my reward on the first day I decided to search for it.

And there, in the quiet, undeserved beauty of the place, my 40-by-40 box starts to look like something more. And the first people through the door do, too. And the voice, in all the calm reassurance of its warmth, sounds like a voice I knew a long time ago. It kept me alive then, when I *lived* in a 40-by-40 box, and was my first clue that this reward I thought I was searching for would be inside me all along.

And then I want to see her and am filled with a quiet sadness because I cannot. So I close my eyes and know this search has ended, and a new search began, and then I feel a supreme hope that one day I will see her face again. And until that day a framed picture of her will hang over the door of this place. And everyone who comes through that door will know: Here is a place where hope lives. Here is a place where we carry on. Here is a place where the reward is in the searching, because life has always been its own reward, and the time spent finding ways to give it to someone else is a search that never ends. And when I think these things and am given to their promise, I am lifted up and carried away with all the hope of a woman born again.

Part Two

Your Story

>Plot
Character
Conflict
Resolution

Six

Plot: Your number is a catalyst

Let me tell you a story.
It's hard to think of six words more intriguing. Since the day we learned to communicate, humans have been telling stories—tales of tragedy and hope; legends of heroism and sacrifice. What we don't see in the world around us we look for in a story. Stories tell us what we have lost and what we have gained; they tell us where we have been and where we're going. They fill in the gaps others leave behind. Stories become the things we want to be.

Stories can take us anywhere, from the inside of a whale to a galaxy far, far away. They illuminate our fears and foretell our redemption. They are the currency of our dreams, the train on which we escape, at the same time unique to each of us and shared among all of us. In the entire universe, stories are unique to humans. They make us unlike anything that's ever existed.

Now let me tell you a story. Every day, every moment, your life is playing out in a plot that you define. Every day you interact with other characters, face make-or-break conflict, and set a course toward a resolution only you determine. Think of any story you have ever read: the rainy afternoons with Tom Sawyer, the sleepy evenings with Jo March. A giant slayer, a boy and his beanstalk. The pirate, the Jedi. Every dynamic character you have ever known, whose only separation from your very life was that yours played out in flesh and blood and theirs played out in ink and paper, only exists because they are part of a bigger story. Now place yourself right among them—because you are, too.

The first part of this book is devoted to telling you my story. But the rest is about you. The idea that your life is a narrative is certainly not a new one; since humans could paint on cave walls they told stories of the world around them. And indeed, whether you see it or not, your life *will* play out in a linear narrative, made real by the elements that make any story real: the plot, the characters, the conflict, and the resolution.

But no story worth telling is simply beholden to those well-worn elements of literature. Real stories have an almost magical way of coming *alive*. The secret I found to making that happen in my story was a number I wore on my heart—a moment I could come back to when I needed it—that motivated me and pushed me and elevated me the rest of my life, which someone birthed inside me. It's the thing that makes me a Number Person.

When you identify the number you carry—your own 1907, in other words—the entire trajectory of your story will change. This number will guide the plot you're on, it will affect how you relate to the characters you meet, it will help you face conflict, and it will guide you to determine your resolution. This number will give you hope, afford you courage, and offer you the determination you need to make your life *more* than just a story.

I said early on that every person has a number. I firmly believe this. Even if you don't know it offhand, even if you don't see your life as the same sort of start-to-finish narrative I have told as mine, I guarantee you have this power inside you waiting to be harnessed. This number will turn your life into something more than just the story of a person who lived out his days on earth. It will help it become something that lives on far beyond the date on your headstone. It will make your life legendary. The rest of this book will help walk you through that. And like any good story, yours begins with the very line on which it is drawn: the plot.

In the 2006 movie *Stranger Than Fiction*, Will Ferrell plays an IRS agent named Harold Crick who one day begins to hear a voice that narrates his every move. Harold's boring, ordinary life is thrown on its head by the discovery that he is the main character of a story. When Harold stands at the bus stop one morning and hears the voice foretell his untimely death, he seeks the counsel of the only person he can find who can help him: a literature professor.

Professor Hilburn, played by Dustin Hoffman, tells Harold that as the main character he is the one who determines the story he is in, not the author, and that for a day he should sit in his apartment and do nothing. In other words, the plot needs its character's action to advance and if there is no action then the plot cannot move forward and the story will end.

So Harold takes a day off and doesn't leave the couch—he doesn't answer the phone, doesn't go to the bathroom, doesn't change the channel. He plants himself firmly on a cushion and waits. And the voice, with no action to narrate, is silent. The plot has stopped.

Moments later, with Harold still quietly watching TV, a bulldozer crashes through his apartment wall, tearing his home to pieces. The machine lunges toward him on the couch, destroying his living room and wrecking everything around him. At a loss for words, Harold consults Dr. Hilburn, who calmly tells him what the unexplainable action means: the story, whether he wanted it to or not, continued without him. The world was not going to stop just because Harold did. Harold did not control his own fate.

While none of us has a narrator calling out our every move line by line, Harold's story is a smart picture of the notion of our lives as bigger stories. We are all living out our own plots, day by day, moment by moment. Even if you don't care, or don't recognize it, or (like Harold) don't even want it, we don't control this element of life. It's part of the bargain on this planet.

Each of us has been given a character and the starting points of a story—the root circumstances of place and time on which we can build our character's narrative. Even if you spend every day on a couch watching TV, refusing to answer the phone or reach for the remote, the story *will* continue without your action. You just determine how much of a role you play in it.

A good plot runs through a story like a smooth road. When told effectively, the reader doesn't even notice he's on it; he simply marvels at the things he sees along the way. The beauty of *The Wizard of Oz* is not that we can watch it and become amazed at how the storyteller is leading us through the narrative. The beauty of *Oz* is in the ruby slippers, the yellow brick road, the Emerald City. The plot runs through *all* of these, but it's woven so masterfully that it isn't until after the wonder is over that we realize the story we have been told. It's all too beautiful along the way to even notice.

A story can't exist without a plot. Without this backbone, these beautiful elements of *The Wizard of Oz* are just a pair of shoes and some bricks and glass. But in a plot that brings them alive, each becomes something breathtaking. Plot is the most important part of a story. In many ways it's the most important part of your life.

Somewhere in your life you have a pair of slippers and a pile of bricks. Maybe it's a skill you hold, or a dream you carry. Maybe it's your kindness, or your loyalty. Alone, these things are only worth so much. But with a plot to carry them, they can change the world. And that's not hyperbole. Because I saw a woman do it.

My plot began in a Nashville hospital in 1972. The main character of my story was born an unwanted, unclaimed baby girl in the inner-city with no parents who wanted her and no place that would take her. Her mother was encouraged to terminate her and her father denied her very existence. Now *that* is the beginning of a plot. I would have had to have really messed up to not get a good story out of that one. As you have seen, of course, sometimes I tried my hardest to.

But every year in this country, thousands of babies are born unwanted and unclaimed into poverty. Their parents don't want them and their relatives won't claim them. Given the same circumstances I was, their stories die before they even get off the first page. These babies will never reach beyond their circumstances. They fall into crime, they drop out of school, and they continue the cycle they were born into.

Mathematically, this should have been my story. That I was given any chance at breaking out of it was because of one very dynamic person and a number she left with me that I used to keep my plot on a different course.

Our lives have two possible plots: the one our circumstances dictate, and the one we can dictate. A circumstantial plot is all about the odds; it is determined merely by what happened to the majority of people born into your situation. No matter what scene you were born into, whether privilege or need, the time and place of your arrival put you on a course to live a story people before you had already lived. There were expectations already established for you, things that you were *supposed* to do. You were born onto a treadmill that was already running. And like Harold, your treadmill was going to keep running even if you sat still.

But what makes us different than Harold Crick is that we are both the main character and the author of our stories. We get to live them *and* write them. Remember the choose-your-own-adventure books growing up? I used to love these books because they gave me the power to affect the plot. "Sarah looked under the bench and saw a bag of cash," the stories would read. "Turn to page 127 to keep the money. Turn to page 150 to go to the police." Rather than just be captive to the author's ideas, I could hold some ownership in them. I got to determine whether Sarah did a good deed or got a new bike. At every crossroads, it was up to me to choose where the story went.

Life is the ultimate choose-your-own-adventure story. But the stakes are much higher.

Dawn was born unwanted into poverty. Turn to page 115 to accept it. Turn to page 170 to do something about it.

Dawn dropped out of school because she felt entitled to it. Turn to page 98 to go back to Arthur Avenue. Turn to page 180 to take three jobs and begin the process over.

Dawn lost her first child months after becoming pregnant. Turn to page 120 to accept the fear and the darkness. Turn to page 140 to find hope.

One of these two choices will be the plot our circumstances dictate—the treadmill that's already running. These circumstances will tell us to accept the poverty, to take the easy route home, to just live in the fear. These are the expected plot courses characters like us have lived out year after year. They are the natural decision, the easy choice, the low-risk move that keeps our established plot running.

It's not worth choosing the other plot, we think. It's too hard, too risky, too far over the horizon. I don't want to break the mold already set for my character; I don't want to stand out. I don't have the talent or the personality; I won't see it through. When your plot reaches a crossroads, the natural move is to rationalize the decision and take the easier, more comfortable path. It's just human nature.

I had a friend once who told me about a writing class he took in college. His professor gave him some of the best advice he had ever heard about writing: Whenever you feel your story going along an established path and running on its own momentum, he said, throw an alligator in. In other words, find some way to shake it up. In the day-to-day plot choices we have to make, these alligators come in the *second* options. They come in the harder decisions—the break-the-mold, off-the-treadmill choices that set our plots on a different course. *That's* when our stories begin to burst off the page into something more.

It might be time to dump your circumstantial plot. It might be time to tell the odds they don't control the story you're living. It can hard to break free, and not just if your circumstances were negative; even people born into immense wealth or privilege have their circumstances spelled out for them. But that doesn't mean they have to accept them.

And when it's too hard, or too risky, when you don't want to stand out or don't feel you have the resources, there's a critical tool your character has already been given to help you get there.

The Story Map
Think back to the characters we mentioned earlier: the Tom Sawyers, the Jo Marches, and the Luke Skywalkers. Every dynamic character in literature and film has one very basic thing in common: at their core, each of these characters has a

story worth telling. That's pretty much the first and only rule of storytelling. *Tom Sawyer* wouldn't have been a very good book if it were about a boy who went to school and did his chores. *Star Wars* wouldn't have been nearly as compelling if Luke Skywalker worked a miserable sales job he hated until he could retire at sixty-five on a planet with an ocean and walk his final years away collecting seashells.

Bilbo Baggins, Scout Finch, Rocky Balboa—we only know these characters at all because at some point they made the decision to reckon with something inside them that amplified their plot into a story worth telling. They found something that helped them face a crossroads and chose that second option. In other words, they each found something within them that affected the plot of their lives. Bilbo found courage; Scout found a hero; Rocky found determination.

It's easy for fictional characters to find this thing. All the authors have to do is give it to them. But I want to offer the idea that all these things that make these characters great—all the things that make them *legendary*—are the things you already have inside you. And even if it doesn't seem like it's as easy as someone simply writing hope or courage or redemption into your life story, I'm willing to bet someone already has.

They may not have known they were doing it; you may not have known you were receiving it. But if you look back over the years of your plot that you have already lived, you will find a moment—maybe even a host of moments—along the way you can use to find these characteristics. The teacher who believed in you, the mentor who invested in you, the selfless sharecropper who saved you. The day you walked your first stage, the day your baby was born two minutes from death, the day you opened the doors of your first business. The first step of turning your life from an everyday circumstantial plot into a difference-making story is looking *back* on your plot and identifying this moment. You are a Number Person. And a life-defining plot begins with that realization. From there, you will unpack everything your number gives you. But first you have to find it.

As I have talked through this process with friends at my store, I usually see their faces go one of two ways as I finish my story and ask them about their number: either their eyes light up with an instant realization, or they scrunch their noses and turn their heads because nothing immediately jumps out to them. You may have a transcendent moment that you don't even have to think about or your mind may be completely blank. You may have your own Olivia Witherspoon who changed your life, or you may not.

Either way, identifying the number you will carry with you is a critical step in setting the plot of your life. Even if you have to put some thought into it, it's worth it to get to that point.

You may have already been thinking as you read my story what your 1907 would be. If so, your plot may already be sparked by the hope or determination that number gives you. Even if that's the case, a deeper understanding of that number can help you get the most out of it. And if you don't know what your 1907 would be—if there doesn't seem to be anything that jumps out at you—there are a couple of things you can do to uncover it.

If we're going to view life as a story, it makes sense to approach it like an author. Most great stories are thought out and plotted long before the author fires up the computer. This birds-eye view of the narrative lets the author see things from five-thousand feet, in a sense, and take a zoomed-out look at how everything is going to play out. It helps the writer better understand the characters and their relationships—to each other, to the world he's given them, and to the story they are living. This is a great way to get a look at your own story, too.

Map out the "story" of your life on paper. Write a one-page synopsis with yourself as the main character. What has been this character's story so far? What have been the transcendent moments? Who are the secondary characters and how did they impact the main character?

This zoomed-out look at your story will give you a chance to see everything at once. When you see everything in the same synopsis, these "1907" moments are going to surface in your narrative. See how they show up in mine:

<u>*Dawn's Story*</u>
   <u>*Main Character:*</u> *Dawn Cornelius*

<u>*Secondary Characters:*</u> *Olivia Witherspoon; Michael, Jordan, Olivia, Kristian, and Ezra Cornelius*

<u>*Plot summary:*</u> *Dawn's story begins in an inner-city Nashville hospital where she was born unwanted and alone. When no one else would take her, Dawn's grandmother adopted her and her twin brother and raised them in abject poverty, always investing in and providing them with everything she had. After struggling to get through college, Dawn met the love of her life and with him started a beautiful family that includes their children Olivia, Kristian and Ezra, and their brother or sister Jordan, whom they'll meet one day in heaven.*

Already, in this one paragraph, it's impossible for my numbers to hide. In just three sentences we see that I was raised by an incredible woman, struggled to get through college, and suffered the loss of a child—three life-defining ideas. Once you start to see these moments surface in your own story, circle them in the plot summary and then unpack them further. If I carried this out I would see how much my grandmother affected my past, how my struggle through college was worth it because of her, and how the hope I have found in my family has sustained me. From there I can find the numbers to associate with them. In just a few minutes I can essentially boil my life story down into its own mathematics: 1907, 1992, 1998, 2005, 2007, 2010.

Your life may not be as much of a roller coaster as mine. Lord knows I have experienced enough drama for an entire family. Your plot summary may just be that you were born, enjoyed a nice childhood, finished school, started a career and got married. There may not be any 1907's that jump out of your paragraph. That's perfectly fine. If the numbers aren't hiding in your life story, they may be hiding in the characters around it.

Look again at the list of secondary characters you identified. Secondary characters are crucial to any good story—they bring out the best and the worst in the main character, they set the scene, advance the plot, and give life to a story. After all, who's Tom without Huck? Who's Scout without Dill? Who's Luke without R2D2?

Identify a handful of people who have been influential in your life—a teacher, a mentor, a spouse, a parent, a sibling—and write out how they have impacted you. This is a great way to find your number. My brief list includes my grandmother and my entire family. If I were to write out how each of them impacted me it would be impossible to ignore their effect on my life; and again I would discover how every number, from 1907 to 2010, gives me hope.

Take some time and explore the relationship you have to these characters. You might have a friend or relative whom you feel had some effect on your life but you're unable to pinpoint it. Write a letter to this person thanking him or her for what they have done to your life. List the reasons you're thankful for them and the ways they have made you who you are. Seal it up and put it in a meaningful place where it can remind you of their impact, or, better yet, mail it to them.

Once you go through the process of literally writing out the reasons you have to be thankful for someone, you'll quickly discover what their impact on you actually was. I couldn't write a letter to my grandmother without mentioning the hope and determination she birthed in me. I couldn't write a letter to Michael without thanking him for his courage, or to my children without thanking them for the joy I have found in them. By the end of your letter, you will have thought through all the reasons these characters mean so much to you. And these people who have meant so much to your life—who invested in you and cared for you and spent their days on earth making your days better—will suddenly mean even more.

If you list out your life's plot summary and its characters, if you write the letter and look at everything and still can't find a 1907 in there, don't feel that your life hasn't been valuable. And don't feel that it's beyond this idea. The central goal behind identifying your number is not to quantify your life's value numerically; it's simply about finding something that gives you hope. Having eight numbers is no better or worse than having one. And having one is no better or worse than having zero. If you can't find a 1907 in your life, it doesn't mean your life has been boring or unfulfilled, and it doesn't mean you are ungrateful or not smart enough to find it. Some of my best friends feel alienated from this process because they can't find a number when they think through their lives. But it doesn't mean they can't still find value in the process.

Even if you go through the story mapping process and don't find a number, think about what you have done anyway—you have given yourself the ability to look at your life story, all the major players who influenced it, and take inventory of where you are along the way. Are you happy with where you are? Do you see anything you need to change? Do you see relationships that need repairing? Is there a character who needs a reconnecting phone call or cup of coffee? Spelling your life out on paper is an incredible exercise to do from time to time just to get an idea of where your plot has been leading you.

And if you do want a number but can't find one, fire up your phone or walk into the kitchen and look at the calendar. What day is it? What's the year? It's cliché, but the reality of walking through this journey on earth is that as long as we're here, it's *never* too late to seize *this* moment—*this* year—as your number, and use it as a catalyst to launch your life's plot.

I was talking with a friend after our store opened about her number and the direction of her life. She was generally happy with how things had gone—she had gone to school, married well, and was living in a city that made her happy. Months before, she had recaptured her dream of being a chef. Already holding a bachelor's degree in photography, she enrolled in culinary school to earn a second degree in culinary arts. She had a normal, happy enough life to that point and didn't see anything that could stand out like 1907 did to me.

I could tell she was frustrated that there didn't seem to be a number in her life that stuck out. But as we talked through it and I saw her think, I could see she was entertaining a different spin on the idea that we all hold a 1907 inside us. She wasn't sure what the transcendent moment in her past was, but she knew that over the last twelve months she had made a conscious decision to take control of her life's passion. She had reckoned with her love for cooking, worked to save the money for school, and gone back to get a second degree. The last year had been her year of action. The number that changed her life was on the calendar right in front of her. Her number was 2013.

* * *

Once you have your number and a clearer understanding of what it means to you, the work is on you to apply it to your plot. What will you do with this thing? There's a very symbiotic relationship between your plot and your number; each needs the other to work. A plot without a number is just a pair of slippers, but a number without a plot is just

Kansas. Put together, the slippers and Kansas work together to create magic.

Without my number, my plot was just another girl born into the streets without hope. And without my plot, my number was just my grandmother—just a woman doing what she could to survive. It took both pieces to come together to change my life. I needed the streets to provide the hole my grandmother would fill and I needed her to take me beyond them.

Earlier I said that I was collecting my numbers as I went through life like arrows in a quiver. The idea in that image is that I was packing them away to use later when I would need them. At some point you'll run into one of those forks in the road and it will be up to you to choose whether you take the *circumstantial* path or the *intentional* path. That's when you will need an arrow. When I dropped out of college, 1907 was there, ready to be fired. It reminded me of work ethic and determination and purpose. And it got me back in school. It threw an alligator in my plot. It kept me moving.

When I struggled with my pregnancies and didn't know what the next day would bring, 1907 was there again. I saw peace in her face and a calm determination that reminded me that no matter what the next day might bring, it was always possible to face it with courage and grace. When I could have lost hope, or lost faith, or harbored anger, 1907 was there.

This number you have can offer you so much. These people who birth them in us are such treasures.

They don't even *realize* the impact they're having. You don't realize the impact *you're* having when you offer hope in another person. Because of Olivia Witherspoon, I have been able to keep a simple four-digit number in my back pocket that I can pull out whenever I need a shot of courage or hope or grace or kindness or love. When I need to be reminded why life is worth living, or why it was worth it to leave my job and try to create even just a little impact, 1907 offers that.

I'm not telling you this to brag on her or me. I'm telling you because I want you to feel the urgency in this idea. Life is short. Here I just feel like I got started and I'm already halfway through. If you are struggling with a relationship, with reconciliation, with faith, with your job, with *anything*, it is worth it to explore what your number is, because it can breathe fresh life into your plot. It can rattle off the dust you have allowed to settle.

It's important to remember something about this idea, though. Your story might not mean quitting your job or moving, though it might. Life isn't necessarily all-or-nothing. It doesn't have to mean starting a business or selling all your possessions. Remember the little stories that built yours—remember my grandmother's story. She didn't move to Africa or give away all her possessions. She gardened and made cornbread. She knitted. Not every moment is going to be a titanic one. Olivia Witherspoon just did what she felt was right. She didn't know the sparks she was lighting.

Little things matter. So take that pressure off yourself. You don't have to stay up until 3 a.m. racking your brain with what your next big change-the-world idea is going to be. You might just need to invite one of your kids' friends over for dinner one night. You might need to go to that soup kitchen after all. If you're using your number to do what feels right, the world will change along with it. How can it not? When we're all a little nicer, a little braver, a little more principled, this place isn't going to stay the same. It won't be able to.

Identifying your number isn't necessarily about packing it away until the "big thing" comes along and you make a dramatic decision to move to India or quit your job. Not all of us can do that. It's about living your life. It's about the little moments. It's about the woman at work that needs a cup of coffee. It's about the nursery that needs a volunteer. It's about that first night after your child moves out that feels a little longer than the others. These are plot-points that might need a little help. And when you have something inside that can offer it, you'll find a story that refuses to get bogged down in the hard stuff.

So here we have a world where everyone has been given a chance to live their own plot and a life where we all have a chance to live them with impact. Some of us will squander it; some of us will conquer it. Some of us will endure; some of us will thrive. Some of us only care about today; some of us will change the world.

The important thing to remember is that on Day One each of us is given the same gift: a blank plot ready to be turned into a story. I believe along the way you'll get a number—or many numbers—that will propel this story. Whether you recognize it or not, you are a character in your own story, like all the great characters of literature, with the chance to make the most of the story you're living.

But what makes this better than literature is that unlike Scout and Bilbo and Harold Crick, we are not in an isolated universe. Each of those characters was limited by his own world that was created for him. We share the *same* story. Imagine if Bilbo Baggins and Scout Finch and Luke Skywalker all inhabited the same story, with Bilbo's courage, Scout's resolve, and Luke's sense of calling. Imagine the world they would create. Imagine the plots they would discover, the characters they would interact with, the conflicts they could overcome. Imagine that universe!

We share a planet with 7 billion other amazing characters, all intertwined in the same story universe. Our author has already given this power of possibility, this chance to change the world—to us.

We are the Number People and we have a secret weapon that can shape our narratives. We have a different definition of plot: not the words between "Once upon a time" and "The end," but the real, every day, ground-shifting choices we make when our feet hit the floor. You are a Number Person. We are the Number People. And there are more of us than you think.

Plot
>Character
Conflict
Resolution

Seven

Character: Your number changes your relationships

You didn't see it coming.
Monday morning started like any other—you climbed out of bed at 6:30, took in your usual cups of coffee, and hopped in the shower. Your presentation for the meeting at work was about ready. It's going to be nice to get it over with. Are the kids up yet?
You need to remember to organize the volunteers for the PTA garage sale next weekend...and there's mom's birthday in a few days; you must call the florist this afternoon. Do you have enough eggs to get through the week? Is the rain going to hold off for Little League tonight? You need to have dinner ready early if not. Oh and you must get gas before you go to

work—though maybe you have enough to hold you over until lunch. Lunch. Are there leftovers from last night or will you have to grab something? Maybe there's--

And then you feel it. Unmistakably. Undeniably. Your fingers trace over a lump.

Your heart skips. Slowly you turn off the water and walk out, get dressed, and call your doctor. He can see you at noon. Quietly you grab a granola bar and float out, dropping the kids off with a smile and coasting through the meeting. You can't focus. It's probably nothing, you know—maybe these things are stress related or something to do with allergies. Your co-worker notices something's on your mind, but you brush it off. "Oh it's nothing," you say. "Just a little stress. But I'll be fine."

The doctor does some blood work and runs a few tests. "It could be some different things," he says, "but we won't know for sure for a few days." He gives you the names of two specialists, just in case, but tells you to go home and go on with your routine.

Tuesday passes, then Wednesday. You're back in the shower again Thursday when the phone rings in the bedroom. Slowly you turn off the water again and walk to the bedroom. You take a deep breath when you see the number on the screen. He wants you to come in that morning if you can. And he gives you the numbers of a few more specialists.

After more tests, more blood work, and more unknown, the doctors tell you they have a feeling they can't seem to shake. The lump is painful now, and needs to be treated aggressively. Little League gets rained out. Your mother's birthday passes. You lose your hair. The lump remains.

Soon the doctors give you the word: Two years, best-case scenario.

Seven-hundred and thirty days. That's what you have left.

What do you do?

* * *

My best friend faced this question in 2001. Clarice was one of the best pictures of an authentic life I have ever known—brave, confident, and full of joy. We became friends accidentally. She didn't like me at first when I started work on staff with her at a church in 1999—I was the new hotshot with big plans to shake up how everything was being done—and I had to win over her confidence. I loved that about her. I had to *earn* my way into her trust. Not because she was distrusting or rude, but because when she loved somebody she loved them fiercely and only a few of us really knew her or her love in that way. There were no half-done relationships in her life. Even though she was eighteen years older than me, we became bonded by a love and understanding that went beyond simple friendship.

I knew Clarice was sick when we first met. One of the first transcendent moments we spent together was early on; Clarice needed a double-lung transplant and asked me to drive her to the hospital to take notes. This became a central part of our relationship. I became the person who went with her into the dark places who took notes and could remain clear-headed in the face of a diagnosis or operation. In 2001, Clarice was diagnosed with primary pulmonary hypertension. The walls of her arteries were thickening and soon blood would be unable to flow to her heart. She was given two years to live.

Clarice decided early not to take any medication prescribed by her doctors which was still being researched and tested for use with patients with her condition. Instead, she sought natural remedies. She was at peace with her life. "The hand of the Lord is upon me," she would say, "and I don't need to be afraid."

The hand of the Lord is upon me. Yeah. This was a brave woman.

Clarice's steadfast attitude gave me strength. If the hand of the Lord was upon her, surely it was upon me, too. And if that was true, then what was there to fear? Life was before us to live. And so we did. Even though I knew my best friend was going to die, I never spent much time mulling over her death. I trusted her courage. I soaked in her sense of life. I believed her when she said the hand of the Lord was upon her. So I did not spend time with Clarice while she was dying. I spent time with her while she was living. And the more we did, the more we noticed calendar after calendar flip over as our lives just...continued on.

With death out of our minds, life filled in the gaps.

Clarice accepted God's plan for her life, but she struggled with how to present it to her children. Clarice's girls were just kids. As her illness continued I would become the bridge between her and Asia, Joi, and Nikki. But in those early days they were young, and I was frustrated with Clarice when she didn't want to tell them her diagnosis. She didn't want to worry them, but I didn't feel we got to decide that; God had already planned that they would have a mother with an illness. God knew they would be able to endure it. Clarice was mad at me that day. But the next day she asked me to help her tell them.

As part of that process I wrote a letter from Clarice that she could give to people who wanted to know what she was going through as a terminally ill woman. This way she wouldn't have to re-live it every time someone asked. Clarice passed the letter out for years. She gave it to her girls as she explained things to them. It was just one of the ways she was intentional about her situation. Just one of the ways she was prepared.

In 2011, I got a call from Nikki that Clarice was in a hospital in Jackson. I got there as quickly as I could from Nashville. I stood by her bed with a familiar feeling from a hospital two decades earlier. My best friend was sick. I wasn't ready for it to be over. But Clarice, in an oxygen mask and unable to speak, was as intentional as I always knew her.

We argued back and forth in notes to each other whether I would preach her funeral and eventually I relented and promised I would. It was sad having lived life so purposefully together for so long and in our last moments to finally be talking about her death. But Clarice died, as we knew she would. She made it to October 17, 2011, eight years beyond her two-year diagnosis.

Clarice always took a bag with her to the hospital. I never asked what was in it and she never told me. I found it shortly after her death and it took several days to find the strength to go through it. I had no idea what I would find inside.

As I dug through her personal effects, I saw some things I didn't recognize. Below the clothes and other odds and ends was a piece of paper. As I began to unfold it, I saw a list of names of friends and family. There was Asia, and Joi, and Nikki. There was me. Beside each was the person's phone number. There were descriptions about our relationships to her. There were details.

There were more notes in the bag. One sheet had instructions for what to do if she stopped breathing. Another had all the details someone would need to write her obituary. Each list was another piece of an intentional plan she had built in preparation for her death.

Clarice and I had spent every moment together focusing on life, but as I went through the bag I realized just how much time she really had spent preparing for her death. She had been completely intentional in every aspect. And as I closed the bag I knew for the first time I finally had a complete picture of who my friend really was. Now I had the full scope of her life. She had handled these things privately; so that we wouldn't have to publicly. We could spend our time together living. And so I determined in that moment that I would never stop.

I decided that would be the last day I was afraid. We were back living in Nashville again when Clarice died, in the middle of my struggle to understand my purpose. And as I began to seriously undertake that struggle and seek out what it meant for my life, as Michael and I journeyed down the road that led us to 1907 Apparel, I knew she had given me a valuable tool to help along the way. Because of how she lived, I no longer had to be afraid.

What would be the worst that would happen if we failed? We would lose our life-savings? I would have to take another job? My ego would be bruised? Minor, minor, minor. Clarice had shrunk every one of my fears into irrelevance.

We could have spent those last ten years together talking and worrying about her death, knowing it was only two years off. But as two years turned to three, and three to four, and four to five, six, seven, eight, nine, and ten, we would have been digging ourselves deeper into our sadness every year. And by the end of it we would have spent a *decade* afraid together. But she wouldn't let that happen.

Failure, money, risk—what was the point in worry? What if I only had eighteen more years to live, and that was *it*? All I wanted was my life to matter.

Her girls did, too. Growing up in the shadow of a mother who would not live was hard. It was a sad and difficult backdrop to live your childhood against. But the things that grew out of it were rich and hopeful. Each of Clarice's girls is now pursuing her own entrepreneurial dreams: Asia is an architect with her own graphic design business, Joi is a personal trainer and HR manager, and Nikki has her master's degree and her own fashion stylist business. In their mother's death they saw an urgency to live. Like me, they saw something they couldn't ignore. And all three have devoted their lives to it.

When you don't know when your last moment is, you treat the characters of your life differently. Every character is a gift; every character is an intentional relationship. Clarice could not meet a person and leave him unchanged. After her death Clarice's church grew as people moved into her neighborhood and learned about the woman who walked the streets with a sense of life. Clarice's number was the day in front of her and it changed how she related to each and every character in her life. For me, it meant focusing on what made our lives together rich. For her girls, it meant finding a life worth living. But every person was a character. And every person got to the end of her story changed. And that's why Clarice's story didn't end in 2011. Only her life ended that day. Her story will go on forever.

* * *

The element of character is intrinsically tied to the element of plot. It takes each of them to make the other great; it takes both of them to make a story worthwhile. A great plot with one-dimensional characters is no better than a dynamic character with nothing to do. Each of them needs the other to really sing. And when both of them click, magical stories can be told.

Naturally, you are the main character of your own life story. You're the one living this plot you're on; you're the one holding a number on your heart. But the trap we can fall into is thinking we are the *only* character in our plot—that we are the only one who has anything to do with this plot and this number. But there are *countless* characters in your story. Even if you're the main one, you have been gifted a planet with an almost endless supporting cast, many of whom will become central to your life. This isn't exactly breaking news. But it's important to remember when thinking of your life and your number. Because that number is going to have a lot to say to how you interact with these characters.

I love Clarice's story because it's a beautiful example of how a brave woman used her number to affect her plot *and* her characters. As Clarice's number was the day in front of her, her mission with the rest of her days was to make the most of them. This had a drastic effect on her plot, because it made her seize every day she had, and we spent those last ten years wringing every ounce of life we could out of the time we had left.

But it also had a great effect on how she interacted with the characters in her life. Because Clarice's number was about maximizing the day in front of her, it totally changed the way she interacted with people. Every person became an opportunity. Every relationship she forged had an urgency to it, because that was all her life was going to be about: *this* day, *this* moment, *this* chance to live. It changed how she related to people, it changed how she treated people, and it changed how she left people. I was a character in Clarice's story and the way her number affected her had a profound effect on me. Because she wanted to live, it made me want to live. Because she wanted to keep going, I wanted to keep going.

Put simply, your number affects the way you relate to people.

If Clarice had not had that number—if she had resigned herself to her situation or not found a zeal for life in her final years—she wouldn't have had this lasting effect on my life. I would have taken her to the hospital and helped her manage her illness, but we would have spent ten years with nothing but sadness. Her ability to project this catalyst on to me changed my life and it changed the life we shared together.

This is what you have to consider when you look at your relationships: your attitude—the way you are—rubs off on people. Whether you are full of hope, exuberant with life, stressed and preoccupied with other things, or distant and aloof, that's going to come across in your relationships. Many characters—the lady at the DMV, the server at the restaurant, the clerk at the grocery store—may seem minor to you and that somehow you can simply flip the page when you walk out. This isn't true. Every interaction matters. You are constantly writing stories on others' hearts. The truth is, if you pay attention, these people whom you may think are insignificant to your life story could be writing something valuable into your life story as well. But others—your children, your spouse, your co-workers, your friends—can't cast you aside that easily. They are inextricably tied to you and your story. The way you act will flavor those relationships.

Think back to some of the great characters you have known over the years. When you first met Luke Skywalker, George Bailey, and Jack Sparrow, you originally spent about two hours with them. Julia Child and Lucille Ball and Mr. Rogers spent about thirty minutes a day with you. Reading about Huck Finn and Aslan the Lion took a bit longer, but you were done with your first introductions to them in a couple sittings—a handful of hours at the most.

Each of these characters calls to mind vivid images, timeless lines, raw emotions, and fresh associations. We still see Luke flying through space, George scrambling for ZuZu's petals, and Jack swinging wildly from a wooden ship. Julia and Lucy and Mr. Rogers made us feel at home. And Huck and Aslan took us to places we had never been before.

And they were in and out of our lives in a matter of hours.

Now think about the people you interact with in your story. Every day during the work-week you spend somewhere in the neighborhood of six waking hours with your spouse, maybe five with your kids. On weekends you might be around them twelve hours or more per day. Remember the impression Luke left on you in just two hours? Every week you have around *fifty* hours with those who are watching you. In a year, that's 2,600 hours...or more than twelve hundred times through *Star Wars*.

Think your story is isolated to your own life? Spending forty hours a week with a team at work gives you more than 2,000 hours per year to leave an influence on them. You can't be around someone two thousand hours a year and not have some sort of effect on them. Whether it's your spouse, your kids, your parents, your friends, or your co-workers, the characters in your life are going to get a very clear sense of who you are. They won't know everything. They may not even know half your story, but just in the balance of time you're spending together they *will* become an audience to your story. They will begin to know it as they begin to know you. And the more they get to know who you are, the more they will get to know the message you're giving them—either consciously, or unconsciously.

When you walked through the plot of your life, the story you found is the story they will be seeing. If it's a story of hope, they will feel that. If it's a story of defeat, they will feel that too. But *you* are the only one who can dictate what they take from you. *You* are the only one who can preach your message to them. This is the power Clarice held, even in a powerless situation: She was going to have a *direct impact* on the main characters of her life. She had a message to get out, to me and to her girls and to everyone else: Life is short, so take hold of it and never let go. Get the most out of it you can. She knew it was up to her to leave her own legacy. She knew she would live on in those relationships.

Number People do what Clarice did. Number People look at the relationships they have been given and find ways to apply their hope to them. They look for avenues of change and then pounce on them, because life is short, whether you have two years to live or fifty. Number People know they have been given their numbers for a reason and one of those reasons is to have an impact on the people they meet in their lives.

My grandmother's story is the same as Clarice's. When she took my brother and I in, she didn't know how many years she had left. She was already sixty-five when we were born; it was impossible to know how long she would have us under her care. So my grandmother invested in us every single day we lived among her. And this number I now hold, 1907, reminds me of that investment.

1907 changes my relationships. People aren't just people to me anymore. How can they be? We were not just people to grandmomma. Because she cared about us, I am to care about others. Depending on my attitude when I wake up in the morning I either view this as a burden or a blessing. But the bottom line is it's my responsibility every day of every year. Because she gave, I am to give.

This plays out most practically in my life through my relationships with the people who walk in the doors of 1907 Apparel. The idea behind our store is that we are a house of brands that create hope, and when someone chooses to enter and discover our message, that hope has to start with me. I have met some unbelievable characters there—people who have *survived* things. People who carry scars. People who never knew the disease they beat or the habit they kicked could be something they would want to hang on to. My number changed my plot by making me want something more—but it changes my characters by making me want something more for *them.* When they leave, I want them to leave changed. And that doesn't come from me; it comes from the woman who birthed it inside me.

On the far westernmost wall of our store is a simple three-sentence Story Wall I have come to see in many ways as the anchor of our entire store. I knew when we were building the store that we would need something there to summarize my grandmother's story, so I enlisted our team to dream up a few sentences that could convey the story behind 1907 Apparel with impact. A few days later we inscribed the story on our wall:

1907 Apparel is based on the story of Olivia Witherspoon. Born in 1907, Olivia walked into a Nashville hospital at the age of sixty-five and adopted two little babies born abandoned and alone. She didn't know at the time she was adopting her own grandchildren. But 1907 is not just about Olivia's story—it's about connecting it to yours.

The Story Wall is the most direct way my number affects my characters. It is the thing that makes people realize they aren't simply in another boutique or housewares store. It elicits deep emotional reactions from people. It draws out tears. Many times someone will read it and then turn to me unwittingly and say, "Do you know these people? Are these children still alive?" When I share my story from there, this number has opened an avenue into their lives I am now allowed to enter with a message of hope. My number is what gets me there.

Walking through this number process is not always easy, because many times there are characters you simply don't want to interact with. There are things you want to ignore. It would have been easier for Clarice to pass the buck of inspiring others to someone else and she would have been *completely* justified in doing so. Her diagnosis was tragic; she bore no other responsibility the rest of her life beyond caring for herself and her girls.

Reaching the people in your life can be as simple as treating them well. Maybe it means helping the neighbor carry in his groceries when you see him pull up next door; it might mean getting out of the house and tossing the football with the kids down the street for a few minutes. Little things matter, because they have a tendency to balloon into big things. And big things are what change the world. So don't worry about the crops—just worry about the seeds. If planted correctly, the crops will take care of themselves.

The reason you have a number on your heart is because someone did something that changed your world. Being true to that, in whatever way you can, is the only responsibility you bear.

Character Lists

I'm a list person. My days are so hectic, and the circles of my life so overlapping, that I have to have it figuratively down on paper, but actually in my cell phone, if it's going to get done. Fortunately, lists are the best way to inventory the characters in your life, and a great way to get a look at how your number can change those relationships.

Who are the people you are spending all those hours with we mentioned earlier, and—at least as important—where are the places you'll meet the people you might not think about as much? This isn't a registry to check off when you're nice to people—it's just a way, much like the exercise on plot, to get a bird's-eye view of opportunities in your life you have to impact people. I'm willing to bet you have plenty you don't even realize.

There are two lists you can use when it comes to your relationships. The first looks at the main characters in your life—all the people you know you interact with regularly. By listing out a few notes about these people you can get a much better idea of the true nature of those relationships.

You can get as deep as you want with a character list. When authors approach a novel or major work, character lists don't just include names and roles—they can spiral deep into what makes those characters who they are. What are their preferences, their hobbies, their interests? Where do they work, where are they from, what do they look like? What are their dreams, what are their fears, what are they striving for? The more you know about a character, the more you'll be able to reach him.

As odd as it might seem to write down all the people in your life you interact with, there is *great* value in it. After only a few minutes, you will have a comprehensive list of all the people you have intentional relationships with and will be able to immediately see things you can do to improve those relationships. Clarice did it, because the people in her life deserved to be treated right. All it took was a name and a couple notes for each person. That's all you have to have, too.

The starting points of this kind of list will look something like this:

Michael Cornelius
Husband, father of our children
Needs encouragement, support, reinforcement

Olivia Cornelius
Oldest daughter, big sister
Needs security, fun, belief, pepperoni pizza

The number 1907 means hope to me. It means I want to pass on hope to everyone in my life. When I look at my list, I see so many ways these relationships afford me the chance to do that. I want to show Michael hope through encouraging him—he can be the type of father for our kids I never experience because he's already doing such a great job. I can give it to him when I support him by telling him his talent and drive is going to create unbelievable opportunities for his children.

Whatever your number gives you—hope, courage, excitement, joy, endurance—these needs you're identifying are little cracks that can allow for it to seep in. Find ways to pass on the thing you have inside you. Find ways to develop the characters you love. Your relationships will become more hopeful, more joyful, more courageous, and more intentional, blossoming in ways you could never imagine.

The second list to make examines people *and* place—it's a list of the secondary characters you will meet over the course of a given day, and it's a helpful list to make from time to time. These characters may not be as important to us as the primary characters listed above, but our circles still overlap for a reason. Number People don't believe in coincidence. Life is way too short for coincidence. The grocery clerk, the cable installer, the woman one booth over who asks for a napkin—each is an opportunity to plant a seed. Each is a character in your story.

In a given day you may interact with *hundreds* of people. And while it isn't practical to affect all of them, it has to be worth your time to at least interact with some of them. So make a list. In the morning, jot down the places you're going—the store, the bank, your kids' school—and put down a tangible list of the places you will encounter people. This may not seem natural, especially if you're an introvert. But you never know who's hurting. You never know who needs a word of encouragement, maybe just a smile, maybe just an honest "How is your day going?" as you pass them by. These secondary characters have all the needs your primary characters have. And even if your lives only interact for a few moments, the little seeds you plant in them can grow into big things in their lives.

This list on an average day would look something like this for me:

<u>Tuesday</u>
Olivia and Kristian's school
Ezra's preschool
Gas station
Lunch with a friend
Grocery store
Meetings with clients

Jotting down this list in the morning only takes seconds. But just looking at it I already see how many people I'm going to be interacting with. Maybe Olivia's teacher needs a word of encouragement. I know I will see people at the grocery store, at lunch, and at other places of business throughout the day. This list looks like the most average of average days. But when I write down the places I'll be meeting my characters for the day, it turns into something much more. It turns into a list of opportunities, for the quickest, simplest moments to offer people hope.

Every day you are going to meet new characters while going through life with the characters you already know. The nature of our lives is such that we will always live our stories among one another. Sometimes that's an uncomfortable reality for me, as some days I'd like to just live my story alone. But we weren't created to be alone. We were created to do life together and the sooner you realize that everybody hurts, everybody needs help, and everybody could use a little hope along the way, the sooner you'll stop seeing the people around you as annoyances, and see them instead for what they are: characters. People. Real, breathing, hurting creatures who are going through the same things you are.

That's the magic of living a story with the characters in your life. This isn't fiction. It's not a movie. Number People have something inside them meant to be given away. If you aren't giving it away to the people you see every day, then what's the point in doing this at all?

* * *

So the doctor tells you it will be two years. That lump is pulsing with pain inside you, a ticking clock winding down to your last morning on earth. You look at him through tears, trying to comprehend how you will tell your kids, how you will go on working and parenting and living. One morning you're in the shower and the next you have been given a death sentence. Two years. No warning.

The conversation with the doctor is long and tearful, but eventually it will end. He will give you a hug and see you soon, and on your way back to your car you will have a moment. As you emerge from the hallway into the office lobby, you see the two glass doors ahead of you leading to the parking lot outside. It's a world you viewed very differently before you came in. Past the roof of your car you see the tree line in the distance, and a cloud of birds swooping toward it. To the left is the highway that leads to your neighborhood and your family. The doctor has just told you you don't have long to be with them. In two years you may never see any of it again.

Your character has just been told her story is ending. But the narrative is not quite over yet and walking out of that office you have a choice to make. At the gas station on the way home a woman will be crying. A friend of your son's will be spending the night, too scared to sleep in the same house as his fighting parents. Your co-worker will tell you in the morning she's worried she might be pregnant. All the stories around you will keep on going. All the characters in your life will still be there as before.

Will you use the time you have left to change them?

You push open the glass doors and step outside. You have two years left with these people and your time with them will be done. I knew a woman who lived this reality. She drove home from a doctor's office with a death sentence and in her resolve she decided there was no way her narrative was going to end just because her character's story would.

She made a hard decision that day. She decided she was going to keep caring for people. But because she did, something happened she never could have bargained for. Because she decided her last two years—her last ten years—would be about changing the characters in her life, she wrote the ultimate story. She wrote the story every writer dreams of. She wrote a story that never ends.

Plot
Character
>Conflict
Resolution

Eight

Conflict: Your number can bring healing

Part of the joy of 1907 Apparel is the chance to form partnerships—to join alongside people who are already doing life-changing work and just grab on to their train as it's already moving. For me, the excitement is compounded—the energy of running my own start-up is amplified by the energy of someone else's, and the feeling is like nothing I ever knew in the corporate world. I love our partnerships. I love showcasing other brands and other organizations. It makes me want to be better, and it reminds me of all the incredible heroes already doing amazing work in the world.

These partnerships often emerge from the most everyday conversations. They're often organic and many times spontaneous, nothing we could ever plan for. Sometimes they fizzle for one reason or another, but sometimes they work. Sometimes they change other people's lives. And sometimes they change mine.

I was introduced to 30 Abes in one of these conversations. One spring morning a woman named Amy came in the store, and after introducing myself and getting to know each other a little, we came to find out that we lived only a block away from one another. She worked for a well-known national radio show. After walking her through the mission of 1907 Apparel, she walked me through a mission that was close to her heart, called 30 Abes, based on the idea that all it takes to feed a child in Haiti is 30 cents a day.

My heart gets particularly pricked by the lives of orphans. I have an overwhelming passion for serving them and great compassion in my heart for caring for them.

As I listened to Amy tell me about their mission, I immediately knew I wanted to do something with 30 Abes. I couldn't leave that conversation and not make some sort of commitment. A major 30 Abes event was planned and to help promote we assumed the responsibility of printing and handling orders for every T-shirt that would be ordered from around the country. The money raised would send more than 500,000 meals to Haiti. To have some small role in that made my heart thump. What happened next would make it soar.

About a month before the event, Amy invited me to travel with her to Haiti to see the orphanage. I had done a lot of international travel and missions work in my life, but never to Haiti. And never to a place in which my new start-up social enterprise was actively trying to impact. I immediately felt a draw there I had never known before. It was as clear a call as I had ever heard. I said yes without even thinking.

There was something fresh about being around so many orphaned children—something incongruous that made my heart sink and leap at the same time, devastated by their lives but so hopeful in their joy. In many ways it felt that we were orphans alongside each other, bonded together by our loss, but there were so many more joyful things we held in common. We shared the most human of human bonds, laughter, and ran and played alongside each other. Yes, we were all without parents. But we were so *human* anyway, loved by an eternal Father who watched over all of us. We still ate and breathed and laughed and cried. We still tried to make it one day to the next.

I left so emboldened by the children's joy. On the flight back I had some time to reflect and journaled my thoughts while they were still fresh. It isn't often I get real, peaceful time alone to myself, and I needed it to reckon with the things I had seen. In one of the entries, among the scribbles and notes, I included this in a journal entry:

I had a compassion for them that was fresh, awakened by my own loss yet also covered over in my concern for them and their well-being as children who need parents to guide them toward adulthood.

While there, I didn't see my loss as much as I saw my gain. I cherished holding their hands, holding them in my lap, playing games on the front porch, teaching them about my ethnic heritage—how I could be brown, yet not Haitian—and laughing about the silliness of what it means to be a child anywhere in the world.

Somehow being "home" has made the journey clearer. A few thousand miles later, I'm so grateful for the children of the Maison orphanage.

"I will not leave you as orphans; I will come to you" -John 14:18.

I'm thankful for the truth of this Word.

I was too engrossed by my emotions for the children I had met to realize the watershed moment they had offered me to reckon with the conflict of my own life. Conflict is a major part of being a Number Person—it's a major part of the story of your life—and it's so easy to bury, to ignore, to gloss over. You can live your whole life and never address the conflict of it. But the truth of life is that as we only know light by the dark, and noise by the silence, we only know hope because we know the other side of it. We know joy because we know joylessness. And we can only know peace because we know conflict.

This is the hardest part of your story to reckon with. This is the hardest part of being a Number Person. It's certainly the last you want to deal with. I love what 1907 means to my plot and I love what it means to the relationships I hold with the characters I'm on it with. But it's not so easy when I start talking about what 1907 means to the conflict of my life. It's not so easy to think about my relationship to my mother and father, or what I would say to them if I had an hour alone with them. It's not so easy to think about how holding an orphaned Haitian boy in your lap shatters your heart into a thousand pieces because you want him so badly to know you understand his life.

The problem with these uncomfortable—often ugly—emotions is that when we ignore the ugly parts of our lives, we're asking for a good story without conflict. But when we do this—when we choose to brush our conflicts aside—we're bargaining for something that can't exist. We're eliminating the possibility for story. Because not only has no good story ever been written without conflict, a story cannot even *exist* without it. You can't remove conflict from your story any more than you can remove plot or character. It is completely, unabashedly, inextricably undivorceable from your life.

But there's something kind of amazing about that. Because conflict? The hard, painful, emotional, impossible thing that happened to you? It can be used for *good*. If you let it, it can *save* you. Because the sooner you accept that you will have conflict the sooner you can use it to propel your life story—to better understand the life you have been given and the things you can do to affect it in ways you never could otherwise.

* * *

Conflict comes in two forms and they often happen at the same time. There is external conflict, or the things that happen to us, and there is internal conflict, the inner turmoil we feel over them. The external conflict Atticus Finch famously faced in *To Kill A Mockingbird* was the challenge of defending a black man in Alabama, but his inner conflict was even harder: What would taking the case, or abandoning the case, teach his children? The same event challenged him in two ways and to overcome it meant overcoming both forms of it.

External conflict can be public, while inner conflict is intensely private. Every kid on my street knew I was raised without parents; only I laid my head down at night wondering why they didn't want me. All my friends could see I had dropped out of school; only I trembled at the fear of my grandmother finding out why. In your life you will face one or both almost every day. You will be challenged publicly and troubled privately. You will be watched out in the open and left to yourself when the doors close.

Conflict will drop in on you like a bomb and grow silently like a weed. It will come without warning and linger for years.

Our human nature is to avoid conflict and with good reason—life's just more comfortable without it. But "smooth seas never made a good sailor" for good reason. We shouldn't look at conflict as an exclusively negative part of life. This is the first thing to understand about the role your number plays here: Conflict can involve the hardest, most painful, most intense things you experience in life. But it's the only way to grow.

Understanding this is ninety percent of getting through it. From there your number can help in the same ways it helps your plot and your characters: the hope, the perseverance, the thing it offers, spurs you on. 1907 gets me through conflict because it reminds me of the conflicts my grandmother faced. It reminds me that there is always hope for the hardest things life can give you. What's harder than raising two babies at sixty-five, on less than $200 a month? What's harder than sharecropping as a family of six? What's harder than watching your kids leave one by one and staying behind?

Among the wet eyes and matted hair of the Maison orphanage, I faced intense internal conflict. I was hurting with those babies. But knowing I had a number I could hold close helped me get through it. It helped me remember the conflicts I had overcome before, with grandmomma's help, and the belief she had in me that I would be able to do it on my own. It gave me hope that one day those children could find a better life. It gave me such gratefulness that I had.

This is the challenge of being a Number Person: When you sign up for this process—when you choose to hold a number close—you are holding on to both sides of it. Because whatever it offers you can only understand because of the other side. You only know its hope because of hopelessness; you only know its bravery because of what there was to fear; you only know its joy because of the sadness you have known before. The numbers of all my kids' birth years are such joys, but that joy comes with such an intense sadness I felt before any of them.

But that sadness, with hope, amplifies my joy. The illness you beat amplifies your zest for life. The diploma you spent eight years earning amplifies your self-worth. These hard things can hurt so much. But we only know weeds because we know what flowers look like. And we only know pain because we know joy.

Atticus is a hero because of his external conflict—because he became an outcast by nobly taking Tom Robinson's case—but he only conquered that external conflict because he conquered his *internal* conflict first. He knew what he had to be to his children. My grandmother is my hero because of how she gracefully and heroically handled the external conflict of our lives, but she only got there by solving the internal conflict she faced the second she laid eyes on us at the hospital. Had she not done that—had she waffled on her decision, or put it out of her mind, or put it off to handle another time—we could have been assumed by the state or put up for adoption somewhere else.

If you're stuck on an external conflict in your life, look at the internal conflict that comes along with it. What are you struggling with inside? Find the personal, private thing—the thing that keeps you from falling asleep—and put your number there first.

My internal conflict of feeling orphaned in Haiti was softened by the hope I found when I thought of 1907. From there the external conflict of feeding so many orphaned children was bolstered by my heart for them. Identifying your internal conflict is the first step. If knowing that conflict can help you grow is ninety percent of the battle, knowing how you feel about it is almost the entire other ten percent. You have to solve how you feel about conflict before you address it. You have to reckon with it privately before you face it publicly. Conflict will eat you up if you're not sure how to face it. But if you're confident and hopeful and ready, you can get through it.

The emotion at the root of internal conflict is almost always the same. These feelings that you aren't good enough, that you aren't wanted, that you can't get through it, that you will never change—they are almost always driven by fear. Fear that your conflict is bigger than you. Fear that you will be an outcast. Fear that some conflicts just can't be beaten. Fear is a door that becomes a thousand times harder to close once it's open. But it's at the root of every conflict you will face, in one form or another, and until you identify how it's festering beneath the internal conflict in front of you, you will never be in position to get through it.

But the beauty of being a Number Person is that the numbers you gathered along the way—the arrows collected in your quiver—can be shot right through the heart of fear. They can puncture and wound fear and bleed it dry with the hope and the bravery and the perseverance you hold. 1907 and every other number I have can *kill* fear if I let them. But first I have to know what I'm killing.

The Timeline

The best way to get a handle on the conflict in your life is to get a look at *all* the conflict in your life—to construct a timeline of your story and highlight the major conflicts you have faced along the way. When you see them spelled out, you may notice undercurrents that flow through all of them—similar emotions and feelings maybe even born from the same event that are causing conflicts to pop up time and time again.

As we did with the story map and character list, we can use your timeline to see how your life story is shaped by its conflict. So the first step is to list them out, left to right. If I were to put together a timeline of my character's story that included many of the major conflicts in this book, it would look something like this:

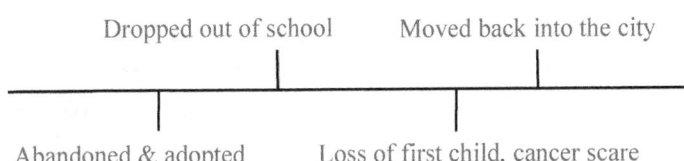

Your conflicts will look very different from mine. They might involve damaged relationships, major decisions you struggled with, hurtful words from your past, or personal decisions you regret. The important thing is to find a way to look at the things that have challenged you. From Abraham Lincoln to Harry Potter, from Earnest Hemingway to Martin Luther King, every person is challenged by conflict throughout his or her life. You may need more than one line to get it all down. But take a few minutes, think over the years of your life, and write it down.

From there, if I look at my line, I notice a few interesting things. First, my conflicts have been external *and* internal—a good sign that something that happened to me (externally) is speaking into the things I fear (internally). And if I dig deeper, it jumps right out: my internal conflicts of raising my kids in the city and feeling orphaned in Haiti are driven by the external conflict I faced of being abandoned by my parents. If you look over your life and the conflicts you remember are external and internal, there's a good chance that the external conflict you faced is affecting you internally. In other words, you might still be afraid of the thing that already happened to you.

Second, I can see that pretty much all of my conflicts are all rooted in fear. Each of my kids' births brought fear in the most harrowing way because of what I went through with Jordan. When we entertained the idea of moving back downtown, I feared what it might mean to raise three kids there. When I sat among the beautiful children of the Maison orphanage and felt orphaned alongside them, I feared what it meant to go through life without parents.

But here's where Number People have a secret weapon.

Think of what I have said I gain from 1907. That number means a lifelong belief that I can be more than I think I can. That I can *do* more than I think I can. It's a number of survival and perseverance and determination and creating your own happy endings. So when I think of these things I fear, and see how they are all rooted in the same emotion, all it takes is seeing how the hope from that number can turn them positive, and these fears change right before my eyes. And then my timeline looks more like this:

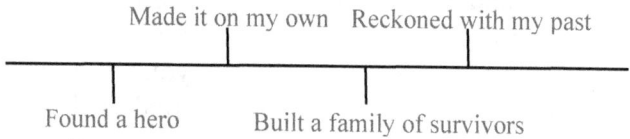

When I look at the timeline of my major conflicts, it can look like I have led nothing but a life of struggle. But remember again: *every* character goes through conflict. Every story endures it. Conflict looms in every life and every life story like a thunderstorm in the distance you have no choice but to drive through. You have to have conflict in order to have a story. So don't fear it. Identify it. Face it. Don't bury it. The most beautiful things can rise out of conflict. None of the discoveries above could have happened if there hadn't been conflict. In every time in my life where I grew, it was only because there was some challenge that shaped me.

But that isn't to minimize the thing that has happened to you. If someone had told me in the days after I lost Jordan, "Dawn, *everybody* goes through conflict," it would have shattered what was left of my already broken heart. There are some things in life that are unexplainably painful, things that take us places we never should have to go. There are still days, a decade on, I ask why I had to lose a baby before I could have three more, and I never hear an answer. I know I will forever be changed because of that. It's almost laughable to call these things "conflict." They transcend any label we could give them.

But, no matter the things you have endured, there will come a moment when enough time has passed that you can begin to reckon with your pain, one little piece at a time. It will come in the quiet of morning, when you walk past the window and for the first time in months notice the flutter of the lark or the warm beat of sunshine on your cheek. It will be in the cool of evening, when your leg catches a row of dandelions, or your hand draws a passing firefly. You can't know for sure when this moment is coming. But life has a way of telling us it's time, a way of drawing us into its own healing, and in the middle of all of your pain and weight and unanswerable questions, you will feel a moment and know: healing, even in the most minuscule ways, is always possible.

In this moment, remember the thing your number gives you. Remember the hope or the bravery or the perseverance—remember the people that birthed it in you, believed in you, loved you, and remember how triumph is possible.

You may not heal all at once. You may never fully heal. But if you can at all, even if it only means you hear the birds and feel the sun, use these moments to remember the beauty that still exists in the world—the beauty that exists in regeneration, in rebirth, in things born anew. Remember you are not alone. Remember no pain is beyond healing. And remember that no one—no matter their pain—is beyond saving.

* * *

When we were in delivery with Olivia, as I was lying on my back watching her vitals drop minute by minute, I had a vicious conflict with God.

See, a faith system is central to the idea of being a Number Person. You have to believe in something greater than the day-to-day for it to make sense. You have to believe there's *more* for hope to mean something. My faith has sustained me through some of the darkest times in my life. But as the doctors were cutting me open, as I thought I might be losing my second child in a row, I got *angry* with my faith system. I got angry with God.

I had wanted to put that loss behind us so badly, to just be in the moment and birth a baby and start our lives together, but when it looked like she might be gone, I told God I didn't know if I could hang on to Him if things went bad. I didn't know if I had anything left in me. I didn't feel like I did. It was one of the tensest moments of my life. If we had lost her, I don't know what I would have done. I don't know how my life would have gone.

1907 was the year my hope was born, and in Olivia's birth 2005 was the year my hope was reborn. I don't think about 2003 as a number, because I don't take power from it. I chose to believe God was sovereign in our loss, but I never got to the point where I felt He was right to do what He did. Why would He create life just to take it away? I made peace because I believe God is sovereign and by faith He knows what's best for my life. But I'll never make peace that that was okay.

Most people hiccup when they begin to reckon with the conflict in their lives, because they feel they have to get to a place where they agree with everything that happened to them. But how could you ever agree with abuse? Or rape? Or the loss of a child? You'll never find a place of agreement with that. But what you have to do is come to a place where you reckon that God is in control and wills what is good for your life. You have to find answers by faith.

I never had proof that God was in control of my life in the days after Jordan's loss. I was a wreck. My world was shattered. All the evidence pointed that my life had spiraled *out* of control. I found healing, but not empowerment initially. As the years have moved on, I now have perspective and have learned so much from this experience of losing a child. So, when I think of the year we lost Jordan, I think of how valuable and precious and fleeting life can be. I appreciate my children with a different intensity and celebrate the nagging days that drag on and on with one reminder after another to pick up your dirty clothes, to put the dishes in the sink, or to pick up the Legos from the floor along with the days when we rejoice together over a positive and productive day at school.

But I didn't start there. In those early days after Jordan's death, I struggled. I questioned God and pushed my faith to limits it had never known.

This is a hard admission for many people because many times we look to our faith for answers, because in many ways our faith is what *provides* the answers to the questions of life. But when we look into the void and see nothing—when we question what that faith is built on—it's hard to find empowerment there. We might survive the thing that happens to us. We might have three more beautiful kids and love our life and find healing in the little moments. But we may not gleam power from it at the time.

If you look at the world around you and feel that everyone is waiting for you to be empowered by the pain you have endured, stop feeling bad if you aren't. Stop feeling that you're wrong for questioning your faith. Stop feeling that you're weird for not finding the good in the horror that's happened to you. God has amazing plans for our lives—plans for hope, for a future—and as time passes it becomes easier to see the bigger picture and how our pain can be used for good. But that doesn't mean forcing yourself to be happy that you endured what you did. The hard truth of life is that there will be things that happen to you that you don't understand, that it seems as if your faith can't explain, that you won't hear in prayer. Faith was never meant to be our excuse, but instead, faith is our reason...our reason to push through the darkness, our reason to create a new future, our reason to step up and be counted when we would rather lay down to die.

Being a Number Person is not about forcing yourself to choose these numbers. Hold on to the ones you can turn positive. Hold on to the arrows you can fire confidently in the direction of your future to slice a path for yourself. Hold on to the lights that light the way.

Having a faith system doesn't mean having all the answers—it just means having one answer, and sometimes that one answer is all you will have. Sometimes you will wake up in bed unable to breathe because of the pain and your faith won't have a solution. Sometimes you will look into that void and see nothing, and the only thing your faith can offer you is the confidence that somehow, in some way you don't understand, God is in control of what you endure.

Getting through conflict is not about having every answer. It is not about finding the happy ending to your painful past, or being able to see the positive side of the things you have endured. It is not about a one-size-fits-all answer for the challenges your life has brought. Getting through conflict is only about finding an understanding that there is some bigger force out there in control of your life. In some conflicts, like the ones on your timeline, you can use your number to find a positive side and propel your life forward. In others—in the internal conflicts no one knows, in the nights you fight sleep—the word "positive" will always elude you. The word "conflict" will shrink laughably in the shadow of your pain. Healing will be far off.

In these conflicts, know that you are not alone. Know that men and women before you have endured them, and felt their faith slip through their fingers, and fought sleep, and looked past the lark outside the window. Know that the pain binds you to others who went before you. Know that it's okay to not be empowered by it. Know that someone else is raising their hand in the crowd and shouting or maybe whispering, "Yeah, me too."

Know that conflict, in all its forms and degrees, is universally human and that even if you don't have to accept that it's right, you can accept that something greater is happening. Know that a day is coming when healing will be possible.

This book has delved into many of the conflicts of my life—things I have struggled with publicly and fears I have faced privately. While I am so in love with my life, I haven't always understood how it's played out. But I wanted to tell this story of my conflicts to show how they can be used for good. I wanted to walk through the pain again, because 1907 and all the numbers I hold with it *have* helped me. They have given me hope when I needed it; they have empowered me when I felt empty. They have reminded me, in preschool carpools and dirty laundry rooms and dusty Haitian orphanages on hot August mornings, that there are indelible moments we hold that change the trajectories of our lives. There are people we meet who love us so much that they choose to spend part of their lives investing in us.

And when it's hard to see past the two steps in front of us, when the confusion and pain is unbearable, these numbers have proven to me time and time again that faith—in all its mysterious, unknowable, unpredictable ways—*exists* for those moments that leave us staring into the void, when faith is all we have to go on, when we don't even know if it's worth keeping, because faith is okay with that. Faith understands that we want answers. And even if it won't always provide them, faith finds ways to fill in the gaps with things like hope and trust and reassurance. Faith can look into the void with us and watch our baby daughter's vital signs drop moment after moment, and *feel* that we might let go of it, but promise to never let go of us.

Because faith, in all the moments we can't—in all the moments I haven't—endures.

Plot
Character
Conflict
>Resolution

Nine: Resolution

Your number determines your outcome

I'm a sucker for happy endings. I always have been. Maybe it's because I have spent so much of my life looking for one, so much of my life searching for the satisfaction and joy that comes with a story that ends well. That feeling you get at the end of a great book, that melancholy contentment that comes at the hard but necessary end of a good movie—that's the thing I have been looking for. That's resolution to me.

But lately I have been viewing happy endings another way. Lately I have been wondering if instead of searching for my happy ending, I should be searching for something else. Maybe there's another ending that's more important—an ending that tells a bigger story. Maybe my number has been leading me there.

I see this when I look at great stories—stories that stick with me, stories that stay on my heart. These authors and directors aren't concerned with crafting a happy ending. They spend days, weeks, sometimes years, searching for the *right* ending. That right ending is not necessarily the outcome that makes everyone the happiest, though sometimes it is. It's just the one that fits the story. It's the ending that does justice to the characters. It's the place those characters need to be.

On some days—more than I'd like to admit—the happiest ending I could imagine would be on a tropical island, tossing my cell phone in the ocean and eating a gallon of ice cream as the sun goes down. But that's not my right ending. That's not the ending that does justice to my story. That's not the ending that does justice to my number. That's not the ending Number People should want.

Instead of looking for our happy endings, we need to be looking for our *right* endings. Look for the resolution that fits your story. Don't concern yourself with the ending that gives everyone what they want; don't automatically take the road that wraps everything up with a pretty bow. Your number—the thing on your heart—is bending toward a certain resolution, and many times that resolution has nothing to do with everyone being happy. It has everything to do with justice. With perseverance. With impact.

To know what your right ending should be, first you have to know what you want out of your story. What do you want out of life? Do you want to be loved or to love? Do you want to earn or to give away? Do you want to settle in or mix it up? There's no right or wrong answer. But you can't know your right ending until you know your own story. And you can't know your story until you know what your character is yearning for. You can't know your life until you know yourself.

So what are you yearning for? What are you searching for? What's your quest?

There is no one-size-fits-all ending to your life, and no universal right ending that applies to everyone. Your ending is crafted uniquely, independently, particularly for you and you alone. You are the only one who knows the way your life should end. Don't base your destination on someone else's map. The directions have already been printed on your heart, in a simple number someone birthed there. This number can help you find what you're meant to do—big things, and small things. For me it reminds me that there is something bigger to life. The number 1907 means I need to birth hope in others. It meant that I needed to grasp the entrepreneurial legacy my family already held.

That number has led me to a life and a business I never could have imagined only a few years ago. But your number will lead you somewhere different. It will take you to places only you can go. You can live your life alongside others, of course, but even within our family Michael's number has written an ending uniquely tailored to his life. He has a number only he is wearing that will take him places.

A right ending can look like a lot of different things. It can look like a new project or dream where you thrive—a place where, like me, you do what you're passionate about. Or it may mean something much more. It may mean a sense of justice—the unshakeable feeling that there are two babies in a hospital who need to be walked right out of there and brought under your roof. See, we all have things we answer to. We all have a sense of righteousness within us. We all have a number; maybe two, maybe three, and these numbers are not just one-off tokens that we keep within us. They are compasses, maps, arrows, pointing us toward our resolutions.

Think for a moment about your number. Think about the thing it gives you—the courage, the bravery, the joy, the sense of life. Now apply it to your story. If your number reminds you to be brave, what do you need to do to be brave? If it tells you to be joyful, what do you need to be joyful? If it tells the story of your son or daughter, what can you do to change their lives? If it reminds you to seize the day, how are you going to do that?

These are the first little steps of the path leading toward your right ending. I have met people whose numbers birthed dreams inside them to change the world, and I have met people whose numbers simply helped them be a little more optimistic day-to-day. You might be reckoning with a planet-sized dream, or a quiet contemplation. Regardless of scale, know something very important about the number inside you: It was not given to you only to use for a short period of time. It was given to you to use the rest of your life. It was birthed inside you for you to have forever—to get you through the little things, yes, but to keep you on track for the big things, the biggest thing: the ending you are building toward.

Your number determines your plot, shapes your characters, eases your conflict, and determines your outcome. It changes not one moment of your life, but your entire life. And that's why it is not to be taken lightly: because it *can't* be. Being a Number Person is a dangerous commitment, because you can't put your right arm in and take your right arm out—you put your whole self in, from day one, and you stay there. You trust the thing inside you. You know that it's worth it. Even in the dark moments, in the heavy conflicts, in the sleepless nights, you stay on the road and you keep the faith, because the best stories don't all end with a happy ending. And the best characters know not to look for one.

My heroes—from grandmomma to Michael to friends like Christina and Clarice—knew better than to sell themselves out for a happy ending. My grandmother's happy ending would have never involved taking on two babies. Clarice's happy ending would have never been about facing her disease head-on. But these women—all the heroes I have known—knew the difference in a happy ending and a right ending. And they have given me more than they could ever know. They have given me the tools I need to write my own.

*   *   *

It's funny that I'm writing about endings now, when my life is so surrounded by beginnings. Fall is turning outside my window, and the leaves are exploding into their fiery reds and yellows. Olivia and Kristian have started another year of school, and their little brother is chattier than ever. The coffee pot is working overtime. In many ways it's fall as I have always known it, except for one very big thing: Just days from now, on November 2, we'll be celebrating the one-year anniversary of this crazy 1907 startup we launched last year. One year of stories and celebration; one year of joy. One year of change.

And while I know we have only just begun, I can't help but think of our beginning in light of its ending. I have seen the numbers. I have read how more than one-half of retail businesses are out of operation within four years. I know the economic climate of our street and the streets around it. The hard facts of brick-and-mortar businesses in 2013 are that no one is guaranteed anything beyond the day we're given. That we are able to celebrate one year in our community is more than I could have ever hoped.

But the joy I get from this first year has me thinking about our ending in another way—because our "ending" is not when we close our doors. And your ending is not when you take your last breath.

Our endings have another word: *purpose*. And a purpose looks completely different from an ending.

There's something important you need to know about the resolution of your story. Whatever it involves, wherever it takes you, know this: You can't get there in isolation. You can't do it on your own, and you shouldn't *want* to. As you are standing on the shoulders of others, lift up your shoulders for others to stand on you. The point of 1907 Apparel was not to start a clothing store I could be in charge of: It was to link arms with those around me, to plant firmly in the heart of our community, and create a company much bigger than just a store—a company that gives back and takes on a legacy I could pass on to those who come after us. I would have been foolish to think I could have gotten to that ending on my own. The place you're meant to be, the thing you're meant to do, is *all* about community.

And if I need a reminder, all I have to do is think about what's ahead for us, and how integral our community will be for that fabric to come together. I believe with every dollar we spend, we are casting a vote for the world we wish to live in. It's up to you to choose where you want to cast your vote. We want to create a place where you vote for life change.

And so we are not just 1907 Apparel. We are 1907 Inc.—a company that uses commerce as a catalyst for change in the areas of poverty, education, and sustainable agriculture. We use a combination of economic levers to fund causes we care about, but we need our community to turn those levers. We use the profits we create to fund these causes for one reason and one reason only: to create real, lasting, tangible change on our street and around the world. And there's no way we can do that alone.

As catalysts, we empower and mobilize others through the power of story—stories, like Olivia Witherspoon's, that go unheralded and unthanked. Stories that don't seek praise, but that simply seek to do the right thing because it was the right thing to do.

1907 Inc. exists for that change. We live for those moments. We thrive on the feeling that we can help other people reach their full potential and give them hope for a better future. We want to *cheer* when we see others grasp the power of their own stories. When we see regular people become Number People.

And so we are not just 1907 Apparel. We are 1907 Kids—a retail arm that grooms the next generation of Number People to consider the choices they make and to act on those choices.

We are 1907 Media—a print and digital arm that inspires hope, change, and action by giving platforms for others to share their stories.

We are 1907 Events—a place for thought leaders to come together and connect with those are tired of just talking about changing the world, and who are ready to mobilize and act.

We are only just beginning. We have not yet reached our ending—but we know what it will be. We know in order for us to get there we will have to open our arms and welcome the help we are going to need. The decision to go on this crazy journey was a decision to form a new community. I know what that community looks like for me. And it's time for you to know, too.

* * *

I have chosen to explore our numbers through the lens of story, because it's the thing we all share. Black, white, young old, male, female, African, American: *Everyone* has a story. I believe that. I am devoting my life to that.

These stories aren't always happy, and they don't always have happy endings. The plots are winding. The characters are rough. The conflict is heartbreaking. The resolution seems impossible. They don't always seem like stories we want to experience. They don't seem like stories we want to live. But understand: this life, these days we have left on earth? That's the only story you have. And if you don't like it—if it's breaking your heart or robbing your joy—you are the only author with the power to change it.

Your number can do great things if you let it. It can change the world if you unleash it. But know that today, wherever you are, you don't have to swallow this all at once. You can't possibly reckon with your entire life in one sitting. It's going to take time. It's going to take a lot of reflection and writing and dreaming to know what it means for you to be a Number Person. It might take a lot of pain. It might take reconciliation or forgiveness. It might take a breakup. It's up to you to determine what this idea is going to do for your life.

In many ways I'm still reeling with the understanding of what 1907 means to me. I know what it's meant so far, and I can see where it's taken me, but I know this isn't everything. I know there's a bigger story out there for me still. I can't possibly know what it is. I have no idea what resolution I'm building toward. The only thing I'm responsible for—the only thing we're *all* responsible for—is being true to the things these numbers give us. Mine gives me hope. So I choose to create hope for others. If yours gives you joy, create joy.

If it gives you peace, rest in that peace.

If it gives you love, pass it on.

If it gives you courage, be bold.

If you don't know what it gives you—if you don't even know what your number *is*—take heart that you are still living this story alongside all of us. You have a plot as I have one; and characters as we all do. If you can't find a number to associate with the people who have made a difference in your life, that's okay. Find something else—a place, maybe, or an image. Maybe your 1907 is a robin's call, or a cedar's shadow. Maybe it's the quiet bubble of a creek in the shade. Maybe it's a Luther Vandross song. The point is not the system: the point is the association. What's important is that you have a thing that empowers you, whether it's a number or something else.

Being a Number Person won't solve all your problems. That's not what it's about. It's not about looking ten years younger or twenty pounds lighter. It's not about *Creating a Better You*. Really, it's not even about doing what makes you happy. It's just about doing what you know is right. But the beauty of the whole thing is I have found that's often what makes you happy. It's about small steps and little signs. It's about quiet moments of healing as much as it is change-the-world ideas. It's as big or as small as you want it to be. It adapts to you.

It's not a secret, this idea. It's nothing I figured out on my own. It's nothing I created. It's simply something I was given—something we were all given—a gift we all share. A common idea that unites us. A small seed that can grow into a mighty tree.

We live in a beautiful world. But that beauty looks like a lot of things. Sometimes it looks like heartbreak, sometimes it looks like joy. Sometimes I walk in my house at night and see three little faces that turn when they hear the door open and know I could never see anything more beautiful. I want to do good for them. I want to do good so they can do well. My number is determining my outcome, because I have decided that to honor it means going all the way. And if my story ends tomorrow, I'm okay with the last chapter I have written.

It is never too late to consider where your story is leading. As long as you have breath to give you haven't reached the last page. Your past is written in ink, but your future is written in pencil. You can't change the things that made you, but you can determine the things you're going to make. You get to write the ending to this story. You get to look at your number and decide what it means for you. You get to wake up in the morning and hear that robin's call and decide what it means for you. You get to stand in the dirt of your own plantation. You get to walk the stages of your own ceremony. You—you alone—get to make this call.

We share something very powerful when we share this idea. We're sharing a calling. We're sharing dissatisfaction with the way things are. And because together we're sharing a view that there's something bigger than ourselves, you are never alone. We are many.

We are the calm and courageous, the confident and willing. We are the bold and the brash, the doers and the seekers. We are the ones crazy enough to see the story we have been living, know it's not good enough, and shred it for another one at forty, fifty, sixty years old. We are the quiet agents of change, never content to watch the world turn from the sidelines. We are the ones who have watched those before us dip cornbread in clabbered milk, and face crippling disease, even death, and tucked that beauty and pain away in the private corners of our hearts, because we knew we would need that thing—even if we didn't know what it was—again.

We are the ones who have worn numbers on our hearts, on our souls, even if we didn't know it, because someone before us changed our world, even if *they* didn't know it. We see the bigger picture—how hope begets hope and change begets change—

and we want to be *in* that picture. We are never content. We are never satisfied.

We take risks, because risks change the world. We open doors that lead to dark hallways and we boldly choose to feel our way down the hall, not knowing where it leads, not knowing what's ahead, because sometimes life is about the dark hallways. Sometimes it's nothing *but* a house of dark hallways. But we walk them, in faith, because we know we're always just one door away from a room flooded with light.

We are the ultimate community, transcending borders, transcending demographics, transcending gender and income and race. We are the ones whose hearts stop when we see a phone number that ends in 1907, or a grocery total of $19.07, or a neighborhood restaurant at 1907 Eastland Avenue. We are a secret club that's open to everyone. We were founded before any of us were born and will end long after all of us are gone. We are but a small part of a big machine. But together we make the machine move.

We are the ones who face stone-eyed doctors in dark operating rooms and feel our lungs collapse at the words "no heartbeat." We have seen darkness— we have seen a lifetime's worth of darkness—and aren't too proud to say that darkness had us beat. But by faith, a faith that sometimes we didn't always understand, we were able to climb, step by agonizing step, back into the light.

We are not interested in happy endings. We know the difference between what's happy and what's right, and we're voting for the one that creates change.

We win. We lose. We mess up. We are messes ourselves.

We laugh to keep from crying, and cry because we can't stop laughing. We have something inside us that has to come out, and sometimes it looks like sadness and sometimes it looks like joy. It's ugly and it's beautiful. It's personal and it's universal. It's the most private thing we will ever hold and the only thing we could ever share. It's our story.

We were always storytellers, because we came from storytellers. And together we are building to a crescendo. Together we link arms across borders and backgrounds and raise our chins to the sun. We close our eyes in its warmth and sense a peace that feels like healing. We sense a God that feels like a friend. We sense a sacrifice that feels like love.

We are not ashamed of our story. How could we be? It's all we have. When we were six years old, wearing quilts shaped like dresses, we couldn't understand the power we were holding. We couldn't know that one day we would not be children anymore. One day we would be men and women raising children of our own and in the doorways of quiet nurseries and the shadows of sturdy bunk beds we would smile at these children and see the unspeakable beauty of a story that's only gone as far as "Once upon a time."

No, we are never alone. Every person has a number.

Only you can tell its story.

Part Three

A Bigger Story

I think about them on their birthdays. I think about them every day, but especially on their birthdays. Birthdays mean something different to me than they mean to most people. They mean more than some buttercream frosting and a pile of presents could signify. They mean miracles. So I think about my babies on their birthdays, because for each of them those birthdays were hard earned. None of them were guaranteed. And for each of them, I'm incredibly grateful.

Michael and I made a decision early on: our kids' birthdays would be personal celebrations—two-on-one, all-day events with just that child, doing whatever they want to do, eating wherever they want to eat, going wherever they want to go. I believe in the gifts of *time* and *experiences*. So for our children, we give them time, attention, and experiences for their birthdays. I believe these are the gifts they (and I) will have forever. So, we celebrate each birthday for the entire day. Our world would stop on their birthdays, because our world *did* stop on their birthdays. What better way to commemorate it?

Back when Michael and I lived in Phoenix, before any of the kids came along, we heard a Christmas sermon at our church on Mary and

Elizabeth and how God gave both of them the names of their children. Our Pastor, Warren H. Stewart, Sr. had no idea that his message that Sunday was having a profound impact on our family.

And his name shall be called, Pastor Stewart said.

When Zachariah tried to give John another name, God took his speech away. There was an intention in the name God wanted to give John.

And his name shall be called.

If God named Mary and Elizabeth's kids, we reckoned that maybe He wanted to name all of our children, too. So we prayed for the names of our future kids. We would name them what God gave us.

Olivia Dawn came first, in 2005, bearing a name of peace—the olive branch—and carrying a legacy of strength. She was the dawn of a new day for us. She would be the first to start a new line of strength in our family. She would carry the name of the women who preceded her, Olivia, her great-grandmother, and Dawn, her mother. Peace and hope.

Kristian Michelle came two years later, our Christ-follower, our Christian, who we knew would be just spunky enough to need her name to start with a K. Her first name would honor another woman who impacted my life, Christina, and her second name would honor her father. Michael. "One like God." A Christian who is like God.

Ezra Michael-David came to us in 2010 and was born into a world with so much to bear. He has so many legacies to hold. We wanted to fit as many as we could into his name. So his name is Ezra, "God is my helper," son of Michael, who is the son of David, who is the son of David. Ezra has the names of his heavenly Father, his father, his grandfather, and his great-grandfather. We pray Ezra 7:10 over him daily. This boy has a weight to carry.

I tell them all the time that God wanted them to be here. God wanted us to have them. There was no other way they would have made it here. Every night before they close their eyes, with their sheets pulled tight under their chins, I lean close to them and say the same line, the last thing they hear before drifting to sleep:

"I can't believe out of *all* the children in the world, God would give us the *best ones*."

And then I touch their noses and kiss their foreheads and walk out of their soft-lit bedrooms and believe it.

My grandmother would often say she wasn't raising children—she was raising adults. I decided when I had children I would do the same. I see them already as what they will become. That's what legacy is: You see the ending before the beginning. You focus on it with an insatiable passion.

There's a secret you should know about this idea of being a Number Person. There's something you need to realize before you go any further.

This whole time we have been working together to find the number you hold—the thing you have in your life that changes who you are. But this whole idea, this entire concept—it's not about you.

Your number is not for you. Your story is not for you. Your life, your experiences, your conflict—they are not for you.

They are meant to be given away.

I have chosen to give mine away to my children. I buried it in their names, I layer it in my prayers, and I embed it in my very bedtime wishes for them. Everything Olivia Witherspoon gave me was so that I could give it to them. It was never meant to die with me.

And so whatever your number is, whatever you hold inside you that you can use to change your life, don't ever think it was meant just for you. This gift you have is meant to be given away.

That's the secret. That's the thing I believe about my parenting—all the things parents obsess over, all the perfect parenting moves and perfect school projects, and perfectly combed hair and perfectly clean dresses? I don't invest energy worrying about these things. It's not what really matters most in life.

What I have chosen to care about are the moments. I make a big ole deal about moments with my kids. Because Olivia Witherspoon made a big deal about them with me.

See, to me 1907 doesn't just mean hope that I could beat poverty and it doesn't just mean that I had a hope that could change the world. It means that I have a hope to change the people in my life. That's all grandmomma did. She didn't start a nonprofit or travel around the world on missions. She just made soup and bread for two little kids. She kept us warm.

She cared. She prayed. She wiped tears. She was a mama, because we needed one.

And so every Saturday and Sunday morning I will cook breakfast for my kids, because she did it for me. And every Saturday and Sunday morning our kids will eat their pancakes over a family devotional, because we only get so many of those Saturday and Sunday mornings before they're gone. It's a ritual of presence and we want to mark it.

That's the bigger story here. This book, this idea, isn't about my story, and it's not about your story. It's about a bigger story that we're all a part of—a chance, every day, in little moments; to give away the thing we have been given. A chance to mark the moments. A chance to consider our legacies, and to reckon with the numbers inside us, and to find a way to marry the two together. Your number can be an *integral* part of your legacy. It can be the bedrock of it. It has changed everything about how I raise my kids, from the last thing I tell them before bed to the same thing we tell them every year on their birthdays, when we look at them over dinner and recount the story of their birth.

"You were a miracle when you were born," we say. And every year they always ask the same thing back.

"What did daddy say?"

He looked at the nurse, we tell them, and smiled.

"Isn't she beautiful?" he said. "Isn't she beautiful?"

* * *

This world is hurting. All around us, on our streets and across oceans, people need love. They need hope. They need to feel like other people care. They need to feel these numbers. They need dignity and humanity and clean clothes and vaccinations and hugs. There is so much need in our world. But so much beauty. You have a powerful thing within you. I hope so badly that you find a way to give it away. Your children are watching. Your co-workers are listening. They may never know what Number Person means or that you have a year inside you that changed your life, but they will see you cut your neighbor's grass. They'll see you give your coat away. They'll see you pushing your son on a swing set.

I hated when grandmomma would say, "I'm not going to always be here," and I don't say it to my kids with those words. But, I do say it to them in the way I parent on purpose. I understand why she did and in a way I'm glad for it. Because it helps me understand the intentionality she put into everything. It helps me understand why at five years old I was standing on a bucket washing dishes and in summers shucking corn. It adds sadness to the memories I have of us hulling peas in the kitchen and digging up rows in the garden. She was teaching me to care for myself—and for others. She was creating moments that would save my life. She was teaching me to sew and knit and bake and take responsibility, so that I could live my life with honor and see her in the background of it. She made quilts, because that's what you do with tattered pieces. You stitch them together to create something new.

The work we do at 1907 Inc. is in many ways a reaction to my having spent two decades in ministry and not seeing a whole lot of change. The bulk of my ministry was shaping *called-out* people to be *called out*. But I realized not long ago that I was spending my life telling people who are called to be something, to be that thing, when I was the one who needed to act. *My* life was unfulfilled. Nobody was being obedient if I wasn't.

One of the last sermons I preached before launching 1907 was on true discipleship—the idea of selling everything and giving it to the poor. How literally are we to take that? Is it figurative? Christ says in Scripture not to worry about what you eat or what you wear, that His eye is on the sparrow. And we live in a broken world that could be outright changed by us living more sacrificially. At least 80 percent of the world's population lives on less than ten dollars a day. Nearly one billion people entered the twentieth century unable to read a book or sign their names.

These are just statistics until you are the one who walks over the fresh grave and looks the woman in the eye whose child could have been saved with two dollars. She is not a number.

These are just words until you meet the man whose life was saved by his ability to read. He is not a number.

Shouldn't it trouble us when the whole of Scripture is about a God who loves us so much that He would give up everything for us to be in relationship with Him? Shouldn't it unsettle us when Christ tells us He came to set the captives free and heal the brokenhearted?

How are we to reckon with this responsibility?

How are we to answer our calling?

How are we to come to understand our role in this world?

I cannot tell you what your number means for you. I cannot tell you what to do with it. And I don't want to. That isn't the point of this book.

The point of this book is to usher you in to this bigger story—to remind you that in your final moments, all alone or with your family gathered round, after your possessions are divvied up, your assets sold, and your loose ends tied, your legacy will be the last thing you have. In a matter of seconds, in a handful of heartbeats, you will go from a person people know to a person they remember. And all they will have to go on is the legacy you leave.

What will they say about you? How will they think of you?

You don't know when this moment will be. I have always said, "You never know when the *last time* is the *last time*." None of us knows how many moments we have left on the planet but we can all use the ones we have more intentionally, more purposefully, more graciously, more loving, and somehow leave a legacy that will outlast us for lifetimes.

You don't know how long you have. But it's up to you to be ready for it—to live a life so powerful, so impactful, in whatever way you choose, that when you're gone they can't mention your very *name* without mentioning the things you leave behind.

And when they consider these things and gather them for your legacy, chief among them will be something invisible. They may not know what it means, or the power it contains, but they won't be able to ignore the unshakeable feeling that you are not really gone.

You have left a number on their hearts they will carry to the world.

About the Author

DAWN CORNELIUS' story reads like an epic adventure filled with near misses, struggle, hope, courage and triumph. From her life's experiences she has uncovered her life's purpose, discovered the power that lies within and the power of sharing her story. Dawn teaches what she has learned. She has emerged as a thought-provoking communicator, savvy entrepreneur, author and motivational speaker.

She has used more than 20 years of professional ministry and marketing experience that shakes up the traditional and disrupts the status quo. Her social enterprise, the 1907 Company, does the same. This fast-growing social enterprise uses commerce as a catalyst for change. The heart of the 1907 Company was established over a 100 years ago, when Dawn's grandmother was born on a sharecropper's plantation in south Alabama. A portion of every dollar spent with the 1907 Company goes toward sustainable organizations that work both locally and globally to lift up others in these areas.

Named by *Nashpreneur* as one of Nashville's 19 "Superhero Entrepreneurs," Dawn changed the retail relationship in 2012 by involving the customer in the transaction through 1907's belief that every person has a story, and a number, that can change the world.

Named by Good.Must.Grow. in 2013 on their "#GrowingGood List" as one of "15 People Who are Saving the World," Dawn conducts business seminars, workshops, and conferences, in addition to speaking, worldwide on the issues of social change, leadership, spirituality, and finding hope through one's story.

Dawn can be reached by email at: dawn@dawncornelius.com.

www.ingramcontent.com/pod-product-compliance
Lightning Source LLC
Chambersburg PA
CBHW060150050426
42446CB00013B/2757